The Political Marx

The Political Marx

Aijaz Ahmad

in conversation with

Vijay Prashad

First published in March 2023

LeftWord Books
2254/2A Shadi Khampur
New Ranjit Nagar
New Delhi 110008
INDIA

LeftWord Books and Vaam Prakashan are imprints of
Naya Rasta Publishers Pvt. Ltd.

leftword.com

ISBN   978-93-92018-30-5 paperback
          978-93-92018-29-9 ebook

Digital print edition, July 2024

To those who interpret the world

by changing it.

Contents

Introduction

VIJAY PRASHAD

Aijaz Ahmad (1941–2022) guided generations of Marxists around the world in our struggle to understand the world and to change the world. With his total commitment to social emancipation, Aijaz studied the world in all its multiplicity to help orient our conversations and our actions, to drive us to think more clearly about the atrocities that multiplied around us and about the possibilities that remained to establish a world system that was not cruel both to humans and to nature. His books — *In Theory* (1992), *Lineages of the Present* (1996), *Iraq, Afghanistan, and the Imperialism of Our Time* (2004) — as well as the hundreds of essays he wrote for *Frontline* and for *Socialist Register*, for *Monthly Review* and for *Social Scientist*, fought off the challenge of neoliberal ideas and postmodern ideas, frameworks that were not interested in dilemmas of humanity and how these dilemmas might be resolved. In 2019, Sudhanva Deshpande, Moloyashree Hashmi, and I spent several days with Aijaz, talking to him about his life and his work, conversations that resulted in the book, *Nothing Human is Alien to Me* (2020), which he told me was his favourite book. His loss on 9 March 2022 cannot be calculated.

Over the course of the past thirty-five years, I spent large amounts of time with Aijaz, either reading him, editing him, talking with him, or listening to him at his lectures. Over the course of these years and our deepening relationship, I came to appreciate three aspects of Aijaz: his erudition, his wisdom, and his immense compassion. He seemed to know everything, the secret to this being a combination of his vast reading of the empirical realities of the world — histories and sociologies — but also the Marxist training that allowed him to develop a theory from those materials. Marxism, he would say, is boundless because it has to retain its edge as the critical science of our times; and so, for each development, Marxism must itself push its boundaries. There was no sense in being formulaic in one's assessment of the world, since it was more important to enhance the Marxist concepts with the actual movement of history. His erudition came from the reading; his wisdom came from that theory. His compassion was evident in the way he put people at the centre of his analysis of the world system and in the way he communicated his ideas, as clearly as possible, in his lectures and his writings.

Many times, over these years, Aijaz would complain about the neglect shown to Marx's political writings. 'Marx is thought of too narrowly for his economic work, which is important', he would say, 'but his political writings are key to understanding his revolutionary vision'. The political writings are often seen as texts written instrumentally by Marx to earn money, which he often desperately needed, or they are seen as beautiful texts with little connection to his economic studies and writings, as if these political texts are not themselves extraordinary displays of analysis of the class struggle and the mediations needed to understand these struggles. During the pandemic, I spoke to Aijaz on several occasions about reprinting Marx's political texts in several volumes, with an introduction by Aijaz for each of them, so that we would republish *The 18th Brumaire of Louis Bonaparte*, *Class Struggles in France*, *Civil War in France*, and Engels' *Revolution and Counter-Revolution in Germany*. Aijaz was very pleased with this idea, and we had drafted a plan for the work.

When the Indian Society of Left Publishers and the International Union of Left Publishers developed Red

Books Day in 2020, I asked Aijaz if he would participate in LeftWord Books' event, which he did. Then, the following year, I asked him if we could do a conversation on-line to be broadcast later for Red Books Day 2021. Red Books Day is held on 21 February, since it is on that date in 1848 that *The Communist Manifesto* was first published. At the end of the twenty-six-minute interview, we had this exchange:

VIJAY PRASHAD: This was a wonderful conversation. This leads me to believe that we should do a series for LeftWord Books, where we discuss various aspects of Marx. How about that? Should we do that?

AIJAZ AHMAD: Sure, sure. We should do that.

VIJAY PRASHAD: Okay great. Well, thanks for coming to talk on Red Books Day about the *Manifesto*. And, perhaps, what we'll do next is to talk about the three great political texts as we come towards the 150th anniversary of the Paris Commune, which will be celebrated this year.

And so, that is just what we did. We held more conversations on *The German Ideology*, *18th Brumaire*, and *Civil War in France*. When we finished the last conversation on the Paris Commune, we spoke several times about collecting these conversations into a book. This did not happen. Aijaz fell ill. Even when he was ailing, he would call to remind me that we have the 'Aijaz Ahmad Project' to complete, including several other books. We could not get it done. But now, in loving memory of our teacher, here are our conversations — edited by me for clarity.

A Moment in the Progression of Marxist Thought

Karl Marx and Friedrich Engels, *The German Ideology*, 1845–46

VIJAY PRASHAD: In 1845–1846, Marx and Engels wrote a manuscript that settled their accounts with the Young Hegelians, who had entranced Marx when he first went to university in Berlin in 1836 (five years after the death of Hegel). Marx attended lectures by Eduard Gans, who had attended Hegel's lectures and who represented the more liberal interpretation of Hegel's work. In Stralau, Marx joined the Doktorklub, a student group that was wrapped up in a radical interpretation of Hegel, and out of that group came the Young Hegelian movement of 1837, which took inspiration from Bruno Bauer and Ludwig Feuerbach, both leading intellectuals in Germany.

Due to his interest in grounding idealism in the actual movement of history and in his growing commitment to social emancipation, Marx developed a strong criticism of the Young Hegelians. He met Engels in August 1844, they formed a quick friendship, and they got to work against the limitations of the Young Hegelians, first in *The Holy Family* (written in November 1844 and published the next year), and then in a much larger book.

Between the writing of *The Holy Family* and the new manuscript, Marx travels to visit Engels in Manchester and for the first time sees a full-blown industrial city. The manuscript that he wrote with Engels in 1845–1846 both laid out his materialist conception of history and pilloried the Young Hegelians. As they wrote,

> One must leave philosophy aside. One must emerge from it, and, as an ordinary person, betake oneself to the study of reality, for which there is an enormous amount of material ready to hand, though of course it is unknown to philosophers. If one were then to meet people like [Georg] Kuhlmann and [Max] Stirner again, one would discover that one had long since left them 'behind' or below oneself. The same relation exists between philosophy and the study of the real world as between masturbation and sexual love.

This manuscript did not see the light of day, relegated as it was to the 'gnawing criticism of mice', as Engels put it in the preface to *Ludwig Feuerbach and the End of Classical German Philosophy* (1886). That manuscript, Engels writes, 'two large octavo volumes, had long reached its place of publication in Westphalia when we received news that altered circumstances did not allow of its being printed'. It was therefore shelved, and only discovered by David Riazanov of the Marx-Engels Institute in Moscow and published in 1932 as *The German Ideology*. The first part of that text is on Ludwig Feuerbach. We are going to focus on that first part. Why is that part so significant?

AIJAZ AHMAD: The first part on Ludwig Feuerbach is a very synoptic statement of what will become the theory of historical materialism. In other words, there are a series of steps Marx has taken towards that theory, but this is a turning point because until then, for Marx particularly, this is a process of coming to terms with his erstwhile philosophical conscience. And he is developing his entirely new philosophy of history in contestation with first of all with Hegel, and Feuerbach becomes a source of strength for him in terms of talking about idealism and materialism.

So, there is a short phase in which there is a lot of Feuerbach in Marx's writings. His early statements on religion, for example, are almost completely taken from Feuerbach. It is not a Marxist view of religion; it is a Feuerbachian view of religion. It is a critical view, but Marx's own view is quite different. For a while, Feuerbach's writings become a source of strength for Marx. Then, Marx wants to become independent of that kind of ahistorical materialism, which is much closer to a very static kind of empiricism. Marx begins to develop a critique of Feuerbach. After Marx's death in 1883, Engels was looking through Marx's papers and in an old notebook he found a couple of pages in which Marx had scribbled some thoughts. Engels thought that was very interesting and gave it the title 'Theses on Feuerbach' and published it in 1886 as an appendix to his book, *Ludwig Feuerbach and the End of Classical German Philosophy*. That is a text that is working towards what he says later. In these formulations, central to the epistemology is the idea of praxis. Historical action to change the world being the process through which you know the world. Knowing the world without acting upon it to change it is pure idealism. Marx comes to see the centrality of acting in history and upon history. Praxis is at the centre of the epistemology.

Then Marx shifts very quickly when it comes to *The German Ideology*, where the central epistemological category is production. He begins then this whole idea of how history is really the history of production, human beings producing themselves and producing their world. It is through changes in the modes of production starting from the first division of labour, which, he says, is the sexual act, which then produces humanity. The family is the first form of slavery, in which the male member of the family is the slave owner and the wife, and the children, are the slaves. It is very interesting to me that for whatever else slavery means for Marx, it fundamentally means the appropriation of other people's labour. Therefore, later he will talk of wage slavery. That shift from praxis to production; a certain narrative of history; successive modes of production.

Marx is still fighting Hegel, since it is not the Spirit that advances from one stage to a higher stage and so on, and contradiction is not contradiction in thought, but contradiction in thought arises out of contradictions in society. Marx takes up the idea of progression in history through contradiction. What is the contradiction? Not in Hegel's Spirit, but between the forces of production (both the means of production, including machinery, and labour power) and the social relations of production (or the forms of economic ownership of the productive forces, with special emphasis on private property). That is why Marx talks about putting Hegelian dialectics on its head; the inversion is from idealism to historical materialism, not materialism. In my view, he accepts many of the premises of idealism as we find it in Hegel. It is a text in the progression of Marx's thought. *The German Ideology* is a fairly central text before the *Communist Manifesto*. The tentative narrative of the modes of production gets summarised and clarified, and you find an even more synoptic version in the *Manifesto*. There is nothing like the precision of *Capital*, volume 3, where Marx describes the mode of production as 'the specific economic form, in which unpaid surplus labour is pumped out of direct producers', which 'determines the relationship of rulers and ruled, as it grows directly out of production itself and in turn, reacts upon it as a determining element. Upon this, however, is founded the entire formation of the economic community which grows out of the production relations themselves, thereby simultaneously its specific political form'; to get there, Marx had to undergo an enormous amount of the hard work of analysis. For one thing, *The German Ideology* is a moment in the progression of Marx's thought, a moment in which the history of the modes of production is elaborated in a particular way, not yet in the way he will develop it in *Capital*. In this text, he is still dealing with Hegelian categories, the relationship between Being and Existence, material activity and thought, which he develops as the relationship between human practice and human consciousness.

VIJAY PRASHAD: Ernst Bloch shares a funny letter from

Hegel to his friend Major Knebel, written from Bamberg in 1807, when Hegel was trying to make a living as an editor. 'Experience has convinced me of the truth of the biblical dictum', Hegel wrote, 'and I have made it my pole star: think first of meat and raiment, and then the kingdom of God will be added unto you of itself'. Bloch says that the Bible actually says the opposite, although Hegel was probably just joking with his friend from Jena. At any rate, Bloch then contends that 'the Hegelian idea does not always require too much turning for it to show a red lining'!

You made two distinctions that I think are very important to our discussion of Marx's epistemology. The first is between Hegelian idealism that leaks into the work of the Young Hegelians, and what Marx and Engels will call historical materialism. The second is between historical materialism and merely materialism. Can you clarify these terms?

AIJAZ AHMAD: Let me say something to preface my discussion on materialism. German idealism as you find it in Kant and Hegel, in particular, has at the heart of it a reflection on the French Revolution. For example, Hegel's *Elements of the Philosophy of Right* (1820) is a reflection on the Declaration of the Rights of Man and of the Citizen (1789). For Marx, the problem is that what is material and historical is apprehended in that thought as abstraction, as philosophy, which means then that you are in the world of essences, and you are not in the world of actual analysis of real movements of history. It is not that idealism has nothing to do with material history. It is that it inverts it into philosophical categories. That is what is attractive for Marx about Hegel and all his life he says all kinds of wonderful things about him, such as how Hegel was one of his great masters. Marx is always struggling with Hegel, because Hegel himself is struggling with the actual motion of history, which he comprehends in philosophical terms. That's at the centre of the quarrel with idealism.

What the materialism of people like Feuerbach does is that it recognises the substantive nature of material reality, but it comprehends it ahistorically. Nature is nature. The social relations that are specific to the capitalist mode of production are seen by Feuerbach as human relations. He does not understand that nature itself is historically produced; the nature as we know it, we do not know physical nature in the way and shape in which physical nature existed before human beings started acting on it, and that nature itself has a history, social relations themselves have a history, and they cannot be comprehended in a way that freezes them in a moment of history, as if they are eternal. The fundamental category is the historical production of all of these categories, of matter itself;

matter is not independent of human action upon it. It is simply saying to the Young Hegelians and Feuerbach that you are fighting abstractions with abstractions, you are fighting phrases with phrases; as Marx writes in *The German Ideology*, 'they forget, however, that to these phrases they themselves are only opposing other phrases, and that they are in no way combating the real existing world when they are merely combating the phrases of the world'. When you say that earlier philosophy is wrong in this or that way, you just want to replace the categories of earlier philosophy with other categories which are also speculative in nature.

It is the historicising of matter itself that I think is the fundamental distinction between that kind of materialism and the Marxist understanding of historical materialism. I would go further and say that whatever transformations the Young Hegelians made to their inherited philosophy, they are stuck in the terrain of speculative philosophy, which is what philosophy meant in that period of time where philosophy is Hegel. Marx is on his way out of speculative philosophy altogether. Étienne Balibar says in *The Philosophy of Marx* (1993) that Marx is producing anti-philosophy. After *The Holy Family* and *The German Ideology*, texts of this kind that Marx produced before the *Communist Manifesto*, he will never again write a philosophical text. There will be an enormous body of writing — such as in the *Grundrisse* (1857–58) and *Capital*, vol. 1 (1867) — with philosophical implications. But Marx will never do philosophical categories. For example, the chapter in *Capital* on commodity fetishism is the most brilliant historical and decisive reflection on the category of consciousness in capitalist society, which would then generate history and class consciousness. That is not history in the Hegelian sense. That is not consciousness as philosophy understands consciousness.

VIJAY PRASHAD: You make the point that Marx moves from the centrality of praxis in his epistemology to production at the centre. This is a very important point that might be lost without further reflection and elaboration.

AIJAZ AHMAD: Praxis in the 'Theses on Feuerbach' is first of all a central category of Marx's epistemology. How do you understand the world around you? Do you understand it by reading more books? Do you understand it through logic, speculative philosophy, and categories? How do you understand the world? The category there is the category of praxis. Not only do you have to comprehend the world of objects as sensuous objects produced by human activity, but you can understand the world only through praxis. Therefore, that 11th Thesis — 'Philosophers have hitherto only interpreted the world; the point, however, is to change it' — is usually misunderstood. The point is not that you don't need to understand the world in order to change it. It is quite the opposite. It is that it is only in the act of changing the world that you understand the world. So, that's what I mean by praxis as an epistemological category. It is only by acting on the world that human beings can actually understand the world. But what is this world on which you are going to act? That remains contentless. It is still being thought of in speculative generalisations, in that language of speculative philosophy, where it is still trapped.

Marx is working through these difficult ideas. It is not just that the publisher did not print *The German Ideology*, it is also true that the book itself is in the form of notes, jumping from one paragraph to another in order to summarise his thought that is racing through his brain much faster than you can actually comprehend the thought itself, in my view.

When Marx writes about production, he is still, in the terms of philosophy, utilising the epistemological category of production, which makes the world intelligible. Creation of means is the first historical act, and history progresses through production of new needs, and therefore systems of production, to meet those new needs. The history of human beings is a history of production; production itself is at its heart the act of human beings on external nature.

The relationship between internal nature and external nature is condensed in the act of production. What happens in capitalism is that a particular relation between internal nature and external nature is torn asunder. So, therefore, human beings enter into very different kinds of alienation, even from their own production.

VIJAY PRASHAD: Marx and Engels spend a lot of time in *The German Ideology* going after Max Stirner, who had published a book called *The Ego in its Own Right* (1844), a development of some of Hegel's ideas in the arena of social alienation and consciousness. Stirner had developed a considerable reputation from this book, which was a forerunner of the trends of nihilism (and whose writings have been compared with those of Friedrich Nietzsche, who was born during the year when *The Ego* was published). They call him 'Saint Max' in *The German Ideology*. In *The Holy Family*, Marx wrote that these kinds of trends produced 'formulae, nothing but formulae', and that they were a 'faded and widowed Hegelian philosophy'. These formulae of the Young Hegelians as well as people like Stirner did not have any apparatus to properly describe and define the motion of history. They were stuck in a world of categories, mirrors that showed them each other. Hegel, Johann Gottlieb Fichte, and others who were rooted in forms of German idealism had an interest in the world; Fichte's *Characteristics of the*

Present Age (1806) and *Addresses to the German Nation* (1807) expressed an interest in understanding the world as it was, finding a way for philosophical categories to be grounded in contemporary reality. Marx broke with the formulaic sensibility of this 'faded and widowed Hegelian philosophy'.

In the Preface to the *Contribution to the Critique of Political Economy* (1859), Marx writes:

> In the social production of their means of existence human beings enter into definite and necessary relations which are independent of their will — production relations which correspond to a definite stage in the development of their material forces of production.

These ideas are there in embryonic form in *The German Ideology*, written a decade earlier. These definitive social relations have a marked impact on how people see the world and how they act in the world; and then there are constraints due to these social relations. This observation, which is across Marx's work after *The German Ideology*, establishes that consciousness is, from the beginning, a social product. That's an interesting departure from the Young Hegelians.

AIJAZ AHMAD: For Marx, consciousness is always practical consciousness. Practice is always both individual and social simultaneously. There is no such thing as production that is purely individual. And if production is itself not simply individual but social and collective, then there is no such thing as a consciousness that is monadic in character, where the individual separates himself from the collective. But production itself is not individual, if you understand production in that sense, not in the sense of manufacturing of this or manufacturing of that, but the very way human beings reproducing themselves through their action, which is always cooperative and communal.

This is a refutation of the whole liberal tradition, in which the locus of reason, of rights, of consciousness, is the individual. Marx's views are a refutation of all of that. Neither rights, nor reason, nor consciousness is located in any one of us. Consciousness comes out of the kind of collective world in which we live.

There is no reflection on the real world. In fact, there is a reflection on their own time. What drives history is production, relations of production, which are never individual. There was some prehistoric moment when there was some human being who assembled the first family, but that's an ideal world; in other words, one imagines such a moment. Human existence has always been collective. The driving force of history is production and relations of production. In *The German Ideology*, there is a formulation that consciousness seems to be a direct reflection of social relations. So, there's a kind of reflection. What he develops in later Marxist theory, for instance, you refer to the 1859 preface, is a certain gap between economic determination and ideology, where he says that economic science can be determined with scientific precision, and then they name a whole set of things, politics, religion, arts, law, and so on, in short in ideology that human beings become conscious of their reality and 'fight it out'. So, there is a certain gap between reality and the ideological comprehension of it, between economic determination and the ideological. That will come later in Marx. In the early texts, such as *The German Ideology*, there seems to be a direct reflection of economic factors and consciousness. There is a certain sort of identity between Being and Existence, between the material facts and the mental facts, the intellectual facts, between consciousness and practice.

VIJAY PRASHAD: You speak about the development of Marx's ideas, indeed the hard work of analysis that he puts into these texts to develop his epistemology and to deepen his method of analysis of class struggle. I find that the debate over an 'Early Marx' and a 'Late Marx' to be overdramatic, for — after all — most thinkers have phases, and many make breakthroughs in their thought, but there seems to me little need to treat Marx as if he had hiked up Mount Sinai like Moses and returned in a 'later' phrase with the Ten Commandments. Everybody develops and matures in the process of their lives, and many intellectuals grow beyond recognition of their early development.

In this text, Marx develops his early ideas about communism. Those sentences are very interesting:

> Communism is for us not a *state of affairs* which is to be established, an *ideal* to which reality [will] have to adjust itself. We call communism the *real* movement which abolishes the present state of things. The conditions of this movement result from the premises now in existence.

These reflections suggest that our 'utopia' is not unrealistic or idealistic, but that it is indeed rooted in the laws of motion of our times. In his *The Principle of Hope* (1954), Ernst Bloch writes, 'Revolutions raise the oldest hopes of mankind: for this very reason they imply, demand the ever more precise concretion of what is intended as the realm of freedom and of the unfinished journey towards it'. Hope, utopia, communism being the real movement which abolishes the present state of things — these words and phrases motivate me.

AIJAZ AHMAD: Marx is struggling with the word communism since the *Economic and Philosophical Manuscripts* (1844) to make the word more and more concrete. In his earlier texts, the word is not really connected with any political project as such, which is related to the motions of history. Communism is the alternative to all this that exists. Here what he is saying, precisely the logic that he has been following up to this point, is that communism is not an idea, it is not outside the motions of history; communism is something that arises out of the motions of history. This motion of history that we have described as a history of modes of production of greater and greater human collectivity and more and more human control over both external nature and the forces of production that human beings themselves have produced through that.

So, to human beings, communism is a logical elaboration of a future that arises out of the contradictions of capitalism itself. This is what will come in the *Communist Manifesto*. The contradictions between relations of production and forces of production, which create the very crises which need to, for a general reorganisation of the forces and relations of production, supersession of it, and communism arises out of that. Capitalism, as Marx and Engels would say in the *Manifesto*, is creating its own gravediggers. It is not by working out a plan, namely this is what a good society would be like; it is not a question of educating people to the real thing that needs to be achieved. It is something that arises logically, historically, out of these motions of history. That is essentially the movement here, a movement of thought; and it is this thought that communism is actually the highest mode of production that history is tending towards. After the *Manifesto*, they begin to talk more about the kind of organisations that are needed and the kind of political practice that would actually correspond to this real movement of history.

VIJAY PRASHAD: That's a good place for us to pause, as we anticipate the next chapter that will enter into Marx's dissection of the history of Europe — France in particular — after the French Revolution of 1789–1794, when he tracks the movements of the gravediggers as they stamp their feet on the Parisian cobblestones.

The *Manifesto* is a Reflection on the Logic of Capitalism

Karl Marx and Friedrich Engels, *The Communist Manifesto*, 1848

VIJAY PRASHAD: The first publication of LeftWord Books about 20 years ago was called *A World to Win: Essays on the Communist Manifesto*. You have a very important essay in that book called 'The *Communist Manifesto* in its Own Time and in Ours'. If the *Communist Manifesto* reads like it was written just yesterday, your essay reads as if it were written today. In that text, you make the point that the *Manifesto* was largely written by Karl Marx, although it was published as a co-written text with his friend and collaborator Friedrich Engels. So, for brevity, let's just call it Marx's text. You say in your essay that Marx not only wrote about capitalism in his time, but because he understood the structure of what was happening, the inner logic of capitalism, he anticipated a great deal of what was to come next. Could you reflect on that observation, not on the clairvoyance of Karl Marx, but on the fact that he was able to understand — at a very young age (twenty-nine years) and early in the life of full-blown capitalism — the structure of capitalism?

AIJAZ AHMAD: Actually, on this reading, my view is that if you try to imagine that what Marx is saying about capitalism is about capitalism in his own time, you would be wrong. Capitalism was not very highly developed in the time of Karl Marx. The whole global production of steel in 1848 was 70,000 tonnes, and most of it was in Britain. So, the *Manifesto* is not about capitalism of Marx's time, but about *capitalism as such*, the logic of capitalism.

One very important part of that is Marx's understanding of the sheer novelty of capitalism and how big a break it was from everything that existed before it. So much of the text of the *Manifesto*, particularly the first part, is devoted to the exploits of the bourgeoisie, precisely in order to grasp what was really new in capitalism's structure. That is the one very fundamental fact that Marx saw, which makes the *Manifesto* not so much a descriptive book. It is not a description of capitalism. It is a reflection on the logic of capital. And, so yes, in that sense, in this essay in

A World to Win and in some others that I have written, I emphasise very much the philosophical engagement with it. In Marx's time, philosophy had not degenerated into the sorts of technical things that it degenerated into. Philosophy, in his time, was primarily a reflection on history and, to be specific, on the motions of history. So that's one thing. The logic of capital.

Already in 1848, well before the work he did for *Capital*, whose first volume he published in 1867, Marx understands very fundamentally that capitalism is essentially expanded reproduction. It does not reproduce itself. The idea is not to maintain the status quo as it was the case of pre-capitalist societies, but it is actually expanded reproduction, that capitalism cannot survive without expanding and expanding in various ways — the logic of which he grasped so well. Capitalism is expanding the sphere of industrial production itself and therefore expanding the size of the proletariat. It is spatial expansion because the market itself has to constantly expand and national boundaries can no longer contain the logic of capital. Therefore, it must go beyond national boundaries. The increasing need for all kinds of raw materials, even food supplies of the kind that you need in 19th century urbanising Europe cannot met within the resources of Europe, and therefore colonisation and imperialism are inherent to the logic of capitalism. Now, of course, this is not a time when Marx has a whole theory of colonialism and imperialism, but the very centrality of that expansion demands an assessment that brings in colonialism and imperialism, and shows that they are part of the logic of capital.

Then, similarly, his understanding of how the capitalist state is different from any form or mode of governance of precapitalist states. So that there is an intrinsic relationship between state structures and class struggles. That again — for Marx — is an engagement with Hegel, for Marx to try and think through and beyond Hegel's notion of the state, with the bureaucracy as a universal class. It is very, very interesting how most of the *Manifesto* is a philosophical engagement.

The *Manifesto* is a text of its time politically. It is not a text of its time in terms of how he thinks of the structure of capitalism. Marx will be engaged for the rest of his life trying to elaborate and work out the logic that is stated here in such a condensed fashion. It is a text of its own time in its political logic.

VIJAY PRASHAD: You raise an important point about how the *Manifesto* is an argument for a kind of theoretical reflection on the structures of society, on production, on social life, indeed, on the motion of history. This text is remarkable for its prose, of course, but also for its dialectical assessment of that motion, and of capitalism within that sweep of history. This is not a rigid assessment of capitalism, because Marx looks at tendencies, dynamics, and processes that of course become rigid and brutal, but then are confronted by workers' movements and is forced to reshape those structures of brutality.

In terms of the *Manifesto* being a political text of its time, it is interesting how Marx simplifies the political terrain. On the one side stands the bourgeoisie, about whom Marx demonstrates an ambivalence, and on the other side stands the proletariat, the universal class. In 1848, Marx had a philosophical attitude to the concept of the proletariat. Engels had already written and published a brilliant study, *The Condition of the Working Class in England* (1845), which details the life and labour of the working class in Manchester, where Engels lived and worked. The word 'proletariat' is first used by Marx in the introduction to his *Critique of Hegel's Philosophy of Right*, which he wrote in the winter of 1843–1844. There he says that the transformation of society will be conducted by 'a particular class', which he names as the proletariat, and then in the next sentence, he acknowledges, 'The proletariat is only beginning to appear in Germany as a result of the emergent industrial movement'. The proletariat appears as a philosophical idea for Marx, as the universal class, the bearer of revolutionary potential, the one who can call — Marx wrote that winter — for the 'negation of private property' because 'it is only elevating to a principle for society what society has already made a principle for the proletariat'. Reflect a little bit for us on the role of the proletariat in this text and then subsequently.

AIJAZ AHMAD: I think it is important to remember that at the time of the writing of the *Manifesto*, there were less than five hundred trade unions in the world. That's the size of the organised proletariat. On the other hand, the European proletariat is moving across national boundaries. The *Manifesto* is written for the Communist League, which consists largely of German migrant labour. These are elements of the embryonic movements from which Marx deduces the future.

I want to return to the word proletariat itself. Engels makes it very clear in his reflections again and again that by the 'proletariat' at that point, they meant any number of things: pure dispossession, not necessarily the proletariat that was engaged in factory production, but this immense proletarianisation, as you might call it, the dispossessed. Proletariat, in fact, meant even the lumpen proletariat, which was actually conceived of as that section of the proletariat which has fallen out of the main structures of the proletariat. Even those who were involved in the petty business trades. When they spoke of the Paris proletariat, most of those whom they spoke about were not factory workers. So, one has the understand the flexibility of the term for them.

However, at the same time, what he understands very interestingly is that the absolute centre of new capitalism is industrial production. You refer to Engel's book on the British working class, in which he has already come to the conception of an industrial revolution, and industrial production is at the heart of it. So, for Marx, the point is not how large numerically the proletariat is in his own time — proletariat now in the sense of the factory workers, the industrial proletariat. The point is that it is at the centre of proletarianisation. This is where the centre is. And secondly, that as industrial production itself grows, the proletariat is going to grow with it. And, as the capitalist mode of production exceeds national boundaries, the internationalisation of the proletariat will also take place accordingly.

Marx is very aware of the very many proletarian organisations in England and France, and even in the United States. One of the things that is often misunderstood is that line in the *Manifesto* where he says, 'The Communists do not form a separate party opposed to the other working-class parties'. If you read the *Manifesto* closely what is being said is that the proletariat is divided into so many different tendencies and so many different groups that making the Communist League the party of the proletariat would be purely an idealist assertion. What you actually want to do is to create a party of the whole, as Marx put it. And it is only when you have reached the point when you can claim that it is the party of the whole, that you can think of communists creating a party of their own, which in Europe they did not reach that point till the 1880s.

VIJAY PRASHAD: When I went back and read the *Manifesto* again, I was struck by the optimism of the text. I don't agree with the attack made against Marxism that accuses the tradition of insisting on a kind of inevitability. After all, in the second line of the first chapter of the *Manifesto*, Marx writes that there is a class struggle ongoing, a 'now hidden, now open fight', that can lead either to 'a revolutionary reconstitution of society at large' or to 'the common ruin of the contending classes'. This is in anticipation of Rosa Luxemburg's choice for humanity: 'socialism or barbarism'. There no hint of inevitability in the *Manifesto*, but there is great optimism. The proletariat will use the technologies of its time — the telegraph in the *Manifesto* — to create greater and greater unity, and this unity will allow the proletariat to lead humanity to emancipation from capitalism, or the 'revolutionary reconstitution of society at large' (keeping in mind that if the proletariat does not succeed, we can end up in 'common ruin'). How do you read this sense of optimism in the text, and in the Marxist tradition in general?

AIJAZ AHMAD: There are many ways one could look at it. In dreams begin responsibilities, so that's one sort of explanation of that optimism. I think optimism of the kind that you're talking about, not inevitability, is — in a very important way — well-founded. That fact is that just a couple of weeks after the first publication of the *Manifesto*, a revolution did break out and it enveloped what are now thirteen countries in Europe, with the epicentre in France and Germany, with massive protests. The first uprisings, in fact, took place a month before the *Manifesto* was published, protests taking place in Palermo, Sicily, in January 1848. So that optimism that this kind of possibility exists and is coming is not unfounded.

A second point is something that was a feature unknown to Marx at that time. But as we look back, something that has remained a feature of communist politics and Marxist thinking is how to turn the national revolution into a class revolution. The Revolution of 1848 already poses that question. As you remember, the Revolution of 1848, now people call it the Springtime of the Peoples, was really a great moment of national uprisings in Europe. How does the proletariat intervene in what is actually taking shape, both as a democratic upsurge against the monarchies as well as a great fear that these movements will become a national chauvinist movement, country by country. So that optimism is at the same time tied up with a great desire to create a political framework, ideologically and intellectually, for clarification for how to proceed at that moment. Can you grasp this moment? That's the question of the time.

It is very much like Lenin's theses on national liberation, and the formation of the communist parties. The idea that nationalism is real, that the national question is real. If you don't take hold of it, if you don't intervene in that process, you will be sidelined by history. Your real choice is to compete with the bourgeoisie, to defeat the bourgeoise, to take hold of the revolutionary movement as it is developing. It is in this sort of moment that the optimism and the will to intervene really comes in. Optimism leads them to great activity. Marx moved to Cologne in Germany, set up the German Workers Club, published a handbill (Demands of the Communist Party of Germany) and edited the *Neue Rheinische Zeitung*. The optimism led him to act, to believe that you can change history if you engage in this kind of activity.

VIJAY PRASHAD: This is a very important point. I regard

optimism, or what the German Marxist philosopher Ernst Bloch called 'the principle of hope', to be integral to any action for good in the world. When I was in graduate school in the 1980s, during the heyday of postmodernism, there were frequent objections to what was known as teleological thinking, or historical thought that presumed an end (a telos). I understand the philosophical and methodological objections to teleology, so that a historical narrative — for instance — should not be designed around how things turn out, because the end might be contingent on processes that do not succeed and then are left out of the narrative. I accept that important warning against a view of history that only favours the victors, and ignores the histories of the defeated and the marginalised.

But this methodological concern leaked into political thinking, where a suggestion developed that one must not imagine an 'end', even an 'end' called socialism, because such teleological thinking was 'problematic', as the objection went. Indeterminacy was the idea of the moment, which was parallel to the neoliberal idea of the 'end of history' and the general sense that the belief that the world can be fundamentally changed is erroneous. If you have such an indeterminate relationship to the future, if you are not allowed to imagine the end of capitalism, then why would you sacrifice so much of your time to try and make the world a better place. This kind of attitude took away from young people the possibility of action.

We have just published *Nothing Human is Alien to Me*, where you and I talked about your intellectual history, about the various phases of your thinking. But we didn't talk about your relationship to the *Communist Manifesto*. When did you first read it and how did it impact you?

AIJAZ AHMAD: I must have read it when I was a first-year college student in Lahore. I read it at a time when my orientation was already sort of 'pink'. I was not strictly already incorporated in the communist traditions, but I was moving towards that. I got my copy of the *Communist Manifesto* from a very eminent Marxist, communist intellectual. It was that kind of impact. It was not an impact only of the text, but of struggling with the text in relation to discussions amongst people, in discussions with older communists. It sort of blows your mind in all kinds of ways. I was already — from what I recall — interested in the sheer power of the prose. The *Manifesto* is one of the great stylistic achievements of the 19th century. It is a great book in prose. I'm sorry that I cannot read it in German. Eric Hobsbawm says that none of the translations compare to the original.

VIJAY PRASHAD: Isn't that always the case. I very much like the earliest English translation, where the text is peopled with hobgoblins and so on. You make that point in your essay from *A World to Win*, where you say, that the *Manifesto* is one of the great stylistic achievements, and indeed that its breathlessness of description captures the sensibility of what Marx is arguing. That is something that writers consistently try to do, which is to find the unity between content and form, to find the form and the tone to match the content and argument. The content that Marx is trying to convey — the onrush of history — is conveyed in the style of the text — the flow of sentences. It is an incredible book, which has been translated into every living language. LeftWord Books and Vam Prakashan's Hindi version, translated by Subhashini Ali, is particularly lovely for that, and whose first line is deeply evocative — *Ek bhoot Europe ki neend urah raha hai*, a ghost is ruining Europe's sleep!

Well Burrowed, Old Mole!

Karl Marx, *The 18th Brumaire of Louis Bonaparte*, 1852

VIJAY PRASHAD: In 1852, Karl Marx published *The 18th Brumaire of Louis Bonaparte*. It first appeared in German in a 62-page issue of Joseph Weydemeyer's journal, *Die Revolution, eine Zeitschrift in zwanglosen heften*, an informal magazine, as the title suggested, published in New York. *Die Revolution* was begun in December 1851 by Weydemeyer, Marx's old friend and comrade in the Communist League as well as Marx's colleague in *Neue Rheinische Zeitung*. He fled Europe for the United States in 1851, where he set up *Die Revolution* which lasted for the brief period of seven days between 6 January and 13 January 1852, but which was revived by Weydemeyer to carry Marx's text. On 5 March 1852, as the volume was being prepared, Marx wrote to Weydemeyer to inform him about his understanding of the class struggle, lessons learnt as he wrote *18th Brumaire*:

> Now as for myself, I do not claim to have discovered either the existence of classes in modern society or the struggle between them. Long before me, bourgeois historians had described the historical development of this struggle between the classes, as had bourgeois economists their economic anatomy. My own contribution was: 1. To show that the *existence of classes* is merely bound up with *certain historical phases in the development of production*; 2. That the class struggle necessarily leads to the *dictatorship of the proletariat*; 3. That this dictatorship itself constitutes no more than a transition to the *abolition of all classes* and to a *classless society*.

These summations of Marx's findings are crucial for an understanding of the narrative in the text.

The '18th Brumaire' in the text refers to 9 November 1799 in the Revolutionary Calendar of the French Revolution. On this date, Napoleon Bonaparte conducted a coup d'état against the Revolution, closed down the Council of Five Hundred, and crowned himself Napoleon I. The uprisings of 1848 resulted in the overthrow of a long period of monarchical rule that followed Napoleon I (the Bourbon

Restoration and the July Monarchy). That Revolution of 1848 set up the Second Republic in France. On 2 December 1851, Napoleon Bonaparte's nephew, Louis-Napoléon Bonaparte, who had been the President of France in the Second Republic, overthrew the government in his own coup; a year later to the day, Bonaparte anointed himself Napoleon III. Marx uses the term '18th Brumaire' to describe Napoleon III's coup by placing it directly in line with the coup of his uncle.

Marx's political text on that coup of 1851–52 is well-known but in an interesting way. From this text come many sentences that have become aphorisms, for instance:

> Hegel remarks somewhere that all great world-historic facts and personages appear, so to speak, twice. He forgot to add: the first time as tragedy, the second as farce.

> Men make their history, but they do not make it as they please.

> The tradition of all dead generations weighs like a nightmare on the brains of the living.

And these sentences are merely from the first page of *18th Brumaire!* These lines are very well known, but the text itself is not so well known largely because it is a deep text, it is an empirically dense text, it requires careful reading of the historical evidence, written within the conjuncture, to parse out the theory that holds together the narrative. So, to start us off, could you orient *The 18th Brumaire of Louis Bonaparte*?

AIJAZ AHMAD: You are quite right. It is very unknown. And, at the same time, it is very well known precisely because of those great aphoristic formulations at the beginning of the text, and also in the last section, in section VII, where he talks about the nature of the state and also there are some pages on the peasantry. A part of that last section is discussed in Lenin's *The State and Revolution* (1918), his great book which is relatively better known than *18th Brumaire*. Lenin extracts from that section and constructs the Marxist theory of the state from the early texts, such as the *Manifesto, 18th Brumaire, Civil War in France*, and the later texts. He quotes that entire section about how 'the revolution is thoroughgoing. It is still traveling through purgatory. It does its work methodically'. It is where Marx says that all previous revolutions 'perfected this machine', namely the state, 'instead of smashing it', and then Lenin writes, 'The question is treated in a concrete manner, and the conclusion is extremely precise, definite, practical and palpable: all previous revolutions perfected the state machine, whereas it must be broken, smashed'. For Lenin, this and Marx's writings on the Paris Commune are at the heart of the theory of the state. For those interested in Marxist theory, very often the text is known through Lenin's reconstruction of it rather than through the text itself.

More generally, within and beyond Marxist circles, *18th Brumaire* is greatly admired, very much like the *Manifesto* and — later — Marx's writings on the Paris Commune. Marx was one of the great stylists of all time, certainly of the 19th century. Stylistically, *18th Brumaire* is a great masterpiece and its aphoristic opening that you are referring to is part of Marx's great stylistic ability to capture thought in language that lasts for hundreds of years. So, there is that.

But *18th Brumaire* is not so well known truly, because the bulk of the text refers, in fact, to Marx's very careful day-to-day recounting of the politics of those three years in France and a lot of it is so dense with that kind of factual reference that a contemporary reader often gets lost in that, and — as a consequence — stops reading it. The actual text is known very well, but it is not read very much in its entirety.

In my view, there is a very interesting relation between *Communist Manifesto* and *18th Brumaire*, the latter being a sort of counterpoint to the *Manifesto*. The *Manifesto* comes in expectation of the revolution, and indeed the Revolution of 1848 arrives weeks after the publication date of the *Manifesto*, in fact the publication and circulation more or less coincide with the outbreak of the Paris Revolution, which then extends to large parts of Europe, particularly to Germany, but also to other parts.

18th Brumaire comes as a way of looking back from the beginning of the Revolution in 1848 to the completion of the counter-revolution. There are, of course, intermediate texts, especially Marx's own writings on this period for *Neue Rheinische Zeitung*, which were collected later by Engels and published in 1895 as a booklet with the title *The Class Struggles in France, 1848–1850*. Part of the density of *18th Brumaire* is owed to the fact that the readers that he is addressing not only know quite a bit about the events in France, but that audience has already read his articles. So, in a certain sense, reading *18th Brumaire* presumes that you have read the articles later collected as *The Class Struggles in France*, and Marx can just condense everything and revisit and refine arguments that were already there in those articles. That's the general setting of the text.

What Engels actually says much later, which is certainly true, is that the *Manifesto* gives you the premises of Marx's theory, as does the *Poverty of Philosophy* (1847) and some chapters in *German Ideology* (1846), all of which gets condensed in the *Manifesto*. The question that *18th Brumaire* poses and resolves is: Can this theory of class struggle, bourgeois state, capitalist mode of production, and so on, can this very general theory be applied and can you understand the ongoing political processes in any given time in light of how does class manifest itself in politics as the political relations are actually lived from one day to the next, one year to the next. That is what he sets out to show, that underneath the surface, what are the actual class forces that are active; what are the actual class determinations of day-to-day politics and how can you really analyse those and reach the class character of what is actually going on. You can turn around and say that there is no access to the reality of class struggle except through the understanding of how it manifests itself in day-to-day politics.

The other thing that is very striking to me is that the *Communist Manifesto* talks about the very essence of class relations in capitalist society and therefore the emphasis is on total polarisation between the bourgeoisie and the proletariat. In fact, a simplification occurs of class antagonism into two great contending classes. That is how the question of the capitalist structure is posed in the *Manifesto*. That is a theoretical approach, which talks about the essence of a structure. This is very much, in a much more mature way, what Marx does in *Capital*. *Capital* is not a description of capitalism as it works day-to-day, but the very fundamental structure, the logic of the whole. That is what Marx gives you there.

What happens in his analyses of actual politics, what comes through in the text, is the multiplicity of political forces and the multiplicity of class fractions. It's not just that you have a multiplicity of classes, but classes also break into fractions. For example, in his commentary on the peasantry, he distinguishes between different sections of the peasantry, the relationship of the peasantry to the army, and so on. Then he goes into the minutiae of ideological issues that trump the manifest class relations. For example, that the French Revolution finally was both negated and extended by Napoleon. It was under Napoleon that we see the true break-up of feudal property, the stabilisation of the peasantry, and the creation of the small-holding peasant classes. The great majority of the French population became owners of small-scale property and therefore they associated their gain of property with the name Napoleon, and Louis Napoleon plays on that, and how the peasantry thinks of the name Napoleon as the legitimate heir of the great revolutionary tradition, which had broken up feudal relations. How the ideological effect of a particular historical development outlasts its own moment in which that ideology is formed. In that way, what Marx shows is that in his time, at least, how different political parties were representing different, overlapping class interests; how the institutions of the state — the national guard, the army — are connected not only to the structure of the state, as understood in Marx's theory, but also in terms of its class roots. What are the classes from which the army, for example, is recruited; the peculiar relationship between the peasantry and the army; and the complex ways in which the peasantry becomes the French peasantry. There's an interesting moment in the text, where Marx says that the misery of peasant life is such that when one of them goes into the army, the misery turns into heroism, and the uniform becomes the symbol of this transition from misery to heroism, and the peasant starts to identify with the uniform, the 'state costume', Marx wrote, since 'war was their poetry; the small holding, enlarged and rounded off in imagination, was their fatherland, and patriotism the ideal form of the sense of property'.

That is what is at the heart of the text: Can this great theory be used to analyse the multiplicity of struggles that are involved when different fractions of classes organise themselves politically.

Ultimately, this great form came to be known as Bonapartism. In his text on the Paris Commune (*Civil*

War in France, 1871), Marx described this Bonapartism:
'In reality, it was the only form of government possible
at a time when the bourgeoisie had already lost, and the
working class had not yet acquired, the faculty of ruling
the nation'. In *18th Brumaire*, Marx suggests that the state
develops its capacity to crush the workers' movement,
when in fact — by *Civil War in France* — he acknowledges
that new contradictions create new possibilities:

> Under its sway, bourgeois society, freed from political
> cares, attained a development unexpected even
> by itself. Its industry and commerce expanded to
> colossal dimensions; financial swindling celebrated
> cosmopolitan orgies; the misery of the masses
> was set off by a shameless display of gorgeous,
> meretricious, and debased luxury. The state power,
> apparently soaring high above society and the very
> hotbed of all its corruptions. Its own rottenness, and
> the rottenness of the society it had saved, were laid
> bare by the bayonet of Prussia, herself eagerly bent
> upon transferring the supreme seat of that regime
> from Paris to Berlin. Imperialism is, at the same
> time, the most prostitute and the ultimate form of
> the state power which nascent middle-class society
> had commenced to elaborate as a means of its own
> emancipation from feudalism, and which full-grown

bourgeois society had finally transformed into a means for the enslavement of labour by capital.

So, by 1871, the empire of Louis Napoleon found its antithesis in the Paris Commune.

There is something very interesting to me. In the *Manifesto*, this idea that there are moments in which the class struggle does not necessarily end in the triumph of one class over the other, but to the common ruination of the contending classes. Now, in a very strange way, the rise of Bonaparte is relatively that kind of moment in which the various monarchist factions, the various factions of the bourgeoise (the industrial and the financial aristocracy, as Marx calls them in *Capital*, volume 3), cancel each other out, while also cancelling out proletarian power, for now.

VIJAY PRASHAD: *18th Brumaire* is one of Marx's longer statements on the question of class and class struggle, an anatomy of the class struggle. Marx's writings on class here are lucid and fluid, able to capture the gap between a class 'in itself' (the relationship of a class to the means of production, the class position of the people) and a class 'for itself' (the consciousness of being part of a class, the class instinct of the people). There are objective class positions based on the class 'in itself', the social inheritances that relate a person to their relationship within a class to the means of production, and then there are the different ways in which people understand themselves in the world, namely whether they are able to see themselves as a class or whether they see themselves as individuals, members of ethnic communities, family members, but not as people who belong to discrete and contending classes. It is here that the famous sentence appears about the 'sack of potatoes', a term used to say — erroneously — that Marx is belittling the peasantry. In fact, he is precise in his description of the condition of the small-holding peasant. Might be useful to share that entire section here so that there is no misunderstanding:

> The small-holding peasants form an enormous
> mass whose members live in similar conditions
> but without entering into manifold relations with
> each other. Their mode of production isolates them
> from one another instead of bringing them into
> mutual intercourse. The isolation is furthered by
> France's poor means of communication and the
> poverty of the peasants. Their field of production,
> the small holding, permits no division of labour
> in its cultivation, no application of science, and
> therefore no multifariousness of development, no
> diversity of talent, no wealth of social relationships.
> Each individual peasant family is almost self-

sufficient, directly produces most of its consumer needs, and thus acquires its means of life more through an exchange with nature than in intercourse with society. A small holding, the peasant and his family; beside it another small holding, another peasant and another family. A few score of these constitute a village, and a few score villages constitute a department. Thus, the great mass of the French nation is formed by the simple addition of homologous magnitudes, much as potatoes in a sack form a sack of potatoes. Insofar as millions of families live under conditions of existence that separate their mode of life, their interests, and their culture from those of the other classes, and put them in hostile opposition to the latter, they form a class. Insofar as there is merely a local interconnection among these small-holding peasants, and the identity of their interests forms no community, no national bond, and no political organization among them, they do not constitute a class. They are therefore incapable of asserting their class interest in their own name, whether through a parliament or a convention. They cannot represent themselves; they must be represented. Their representative must at the same time appear as their master, as an authority over them, an unlimited governmental power which protects them from the other classes and sends them rain and sunshine from above. The political influence of the small-holding peasants, therefore, finds its final expression in the executive power which subordinates society to itself.

The peasantry does not necessarily understand itself as a class. They are more a 'mass', as he writes above, than a class because they do not have the ability — not in a cognitive but in a social sense — to understand themselves as a class, and fail to be able to develop a common political programme and develop their own political parties. That is the reason why their political energy is seized by Bonapartist factions and used for aims that are other than their own. They are delivered to others not only because of where they work and what they produce, but because of the social character of the French peasantry. It is an error to lift this paragraph and expect it to work for peasantry everywhere, since the social conditions of peasants — differentiated by the size and quality of their land holdings — differs from country to country, and so the social ability of the peasants to build political power is not identical to that of the French experience between the 1789 Revolution and the coup of 1852.

When I was listening to you talk about the relationship of the peasantry to the army and the police, I immediately began to think of the uprising in Egypt in 2011. That was essentially an urban uprising, centred in Cairo's Tahrir Square, but with wider distribution in the urban centres of Alexandria and Port Said. When I was in Cairo during some of this uprising, I recall watching the military and police forces as they engaged the protestors and observing that the conscripts of the Egyptian military came largely from the countryside. There was no Tahrir Square in the countryside, particularly in upper Egypt. These peasants in their uniform, their 'state costume', did not seem to have any link socially or politically to the mass demonstrations in the cities. The other experience that came to mind as you were speaking is the 2020–2021 farmers' revolt in India, the Kisan Commune, as it were. The government of Prime Minister Narendra Modi began to abuse the farmers, saying that they are 'anti-national', and accusing them of all kinds of betrayals. This angered the farmers, of course, but it also had an impact on the army. After all, the soldiers in the Indian armed forces — like the soldiers in the Egyptian military — come from the peasantry, and so these Indian soldiers reacted to the abuses of their families by saying, no, these are our families. Many came in uniform, that 'state costume' mobilised now to display their constitutional right to protest, and symbolically gave the medals they earned for valour back to the government. These two examples are not saying different things. Both emerge out of the anatomy of the class structure in the countryside, and the role of the peasantry to the army, and both show at the same time that the political reflection of these class positions is developed in the conjuncture and cannot be read as if from a static mirror.

18th Brumaire bristles with class struggle. In the Preface to the *Contribution to the Critique of Political Economy* (1859), Marx writes about the distinction between the objectivity of class relations and the subjectivity of class consciousness:

> At a certain stage of development, the material productive forces of society come into conflict with the existing relations of production or — this merely expresses the same thing in legal terms — with the property relations within the framework of which they have operated hitherto. From forms of development of the productive forces these relations turn into their fetters. Then begins an era of social revolution. The changes in the economic foundation lead sooner or later to the transformation of the whole immense superstructure.

> In studying such transformations, it is always necessary to distinguish between the material transformation of the economic conditions of production, which can be determined with the precision of natural science, and the legal, political,

> religious, artistic, or philosophic — in short,
> ideological forms in which men become conscious of
> this conflict and fight it out.

The theatre of the class struggle, Marx writes, has to be analysed both through a precise understanding of the structure, 'with the precision of natural science', and through a supple assessement of the conjuncture, where we 'fight it out'. Marx's interventions here are singular.

AIJAZ AHMAD: For me, what is very important is Marx's recognition that class struggle can be understood only if you keep in mind the various mediations that intervene in the daily structures of political struggle. What happens in the political field is that such diverse forces, some representing the new rising classes, some representing the old dying classes, all try to organise themselves in some political form or the other to have their piece of the pie. In this arena, there are major political forces, what Marx goes on calling the Party of Order, in which the two past, monarchical, dynastic forces are represented politically. Marx captures in a few pages the very long-term struggle in French history between Republicanism and Monarchism as it is condensed in the three years before 1852. He writes about the struggle between the 'true' Republicans and the Party of Order, and how Louis Bonaparte actually plays them against each other.

Class does not appear when you're dealing with actual political struggles of that sort. Class appears to you embodied in the political forces. It doesn't appear in front of you in its own purity and wholeness. It is in those representational bodies of the political sphere, with their own diverse ideological baggage, that you have to analyse it and go through it in order to get at the class content. Class content does not reveal itself to you on the surface. What comes to my mind — absurdly — is Hegel's famous saying that what is real cannot be true. What you see on the surface is not the true essence of class struggle. Class struggle does not present itself, in that book, as class struggle. Class struggle is itself at the basis for these kinds of contentions which you can see, and it is by analysis and through theoretical operations that the facticity of facts can be understood.

VIJAY PRASHAD: You started off by saying that the text is filled with detail, densely described events and processes, and that this is possible to Marx — as a writer — because of the fact that his readers by and large knew what he was talking about, events and processes that are not known to people around the world, let alone to the French. *18th Brumaire* is written in an accordion way, with some sections very dense and others filled with air, theory developed out of the details. What is interesting in the text is that Marx shows us that theory is not just about the big structures and processes, but that theory must be developed out of the different levels of experienced and lived reality. Could you tell us about why the detail is important, and what the role of mediation is in the building of a theory?

AIJAZ AHMAD: Engels wrote a very interesting introduction to *Class Struggles in France* in 1895. It is in that book, Marx's *Class Struggles in France*, that the very facts in *18th Brumaire* are covered in greater detail. In that introduction, Engels says quite in the beginning that when you are analysing facts of your contemporary life, you are bound to make errors, and you are bound to make errors because all the facts that you need to analyse the contemporary reality are not available to you at the same time. 'A clear survey of the economic history of a given period can never be gained at the time', Engels writes. 'It is possible only later, after the subsequent collection and assortment of the material. Here statistics are an indispensable aid, but they always limp behind the event'. So, you are bound to make errors.

I would add to that — that the only way you can hedge yourself against those errors is by attention to detail. It's very easy to apply a formula. But what Marx teaches you is that theory is not something that can be applied to the facts. The facts exist in their own space, beyond theory, namely in the realm of the real. It is composed of great multiplicities and great conflicts, so you can't really say — peasantry is like this. Marx will tell you about the different fractions of the peasantry and which of these fractions represents what, such as what is the revolutionary part of the peasantry and what is not. Likewise, the bourgeoisie has many segments in it. So, all classes in fact exist in the reality of factions, in the reality of fractions, of groupings that different parts of the same class struggle against each other, that in actual reality, there is no moment in which the struggle between the bourgeoisie and the proletariat comes out in a naked form in a direct confrontation. The political organisation of the political field is much more complex. And it is out of that complexity, by understanding it in detail that you get to know, you get access to what is the structure of class determination. In a certain sense, if I may put it in a way that might be confusing, the actual class structure is the Unconscious of politics, to put it in Freudian terms. It is by analysing daily politics that you get to that structure, which is fundamentally hidden from you because of all of that superstructure of politics. How to get from the superstructure to the structure through analysis of facts is what the text actually teaches you.

VIJAY PRASHAD: The text is both an excellent manual to study a Marxist analysis of the relationship between the structure and the conjuncture, and of the necessity of mediations to understand the operation of the class struggle on the surface of politics. But it is also — of course — a brilliant exposition on nineteenth-century France. If you take the four books — *The Communist Manifesto, Class Struggles in France, 18th Brumaire,* and *Civil War in France* — you get the entire trajectory of French politics from the French Revolution of 1789 to the July Monarchy of 1830 to the birth of the Third Republic in 1870 and the defence of the Revolution in the two month-long Paris Commune. Even French conservative historiography had to contend with Marx's characterisation of France in the nineteenth century, so that François Furet in *Marx and the French Revolution* (1988) could not ignore Marx and could only critique Marx by not going beyond him but by sneaking in behind him, bringing Hegel back to do the work. Rather than track the social history of France and the class struggle that motored the history along, Furet seeks the laws of motion in the 'long labour of Spirit in history', which is why Furet — strangely — sees the French Revolution as a 'failure' and not as part of a process that rooted republicanism in French culture and structure. These texts by Marx which are concerned with the sweep of class struggle in France are about that story, certainly, but they are about something more for us, namely they allow us to contend with Marx's method of political analysis.

Beneath all the writings of Marx and Engels on the events

of their lives is the great event that took place before Marx was born in 1813, and that is the French Revolution of 1789 to 1794. In 1843–1844, Marx began to compile and read sources on the French Revolution and began to plan for a book on that remarkable event (his notes are in his *Paris Notebooks of 1844*). Marx did not write this book, but he did write many essays, pamphlets, and books that take up the challenge of understanding the French Revolution and its aftermath. His general assessment was that the French Revolution's beneficiary was the bourgeoisie, in whose class interest an entire new civilisation was born. In 1848, Marx wrote in *Neue Rheinische Zeitung*,

> In these revolutions, the bourgeoisie gained the victory; but the *victory of the bourgeoisie* was at that time the *victory of a new social order*, the victory of bourgeois property over feudal property, of nationality over provincialism, of competition over the guild, of the partition of estates over primogeniture, of the owner's mastery of the land over the land's mastery of its owner, of enlightenment over superstition, of the family over the family's name, of industry over heroic laziness, of civil law over privileges of medieval origin.

The sweep of the changes is represented in the sweep of the language, the old swept away — 'all that is solid melts in the air', as Marx wrote in the *Communist Manifesto*. In *The Holy Family* (1845), Marx has already written of the great class interest of the bourgeoisie, 'That interest so powerful that it was victorious over the pen of Marat, the guillotine of the Terror, and the sword of Napoleon as well as the crucifix and the blue blood of the Bourbons'. Engels later wrote that history moves in zigs and zags, that the old never dies easily but fights to survive (the July Monarchy), but then is defeated again (the Second Republic) and asserts itself once more (the 1852 coup), only to be trounced again (the Third Republic), while the working people persist to move the contradictions to their advantage again (1848 Revolutions) and again (1871 Paris Commune). There is no 'long labour of Spirit in history', as Furet puts it, but there are myriad contradictions that are acted upon in different ways by fractions of classes in a relentless class struggle, the zigs and the zags.

While Marx writes about France, Engels tracks these same developments in Germany. He is — in collaboration with Marx (as is clear in their letters to each other) — writing a set of reports for the *New York Tribune* in 1851 and 1852 on these developments, reports later collected by Eleanor Marx Aveling into a volume called *Revolution and Counter-Revolution in Germany* (1896). Engels, in his great modesty and affection for Marx, signed the essays in Marx's name, so that even Eleanor Marx Aveling —

Marx's daughter — assumed that these essays were written by her father; it was later found that Engels was their author. At any rate, these two friends were tracking the contradictions of the motion of history in both France and Germany at the same time, occupied by the great processes of revolution and counter-revolution. During the July 1848 uprisings, Marx assessed the nature of the bourgeoisies in France and Germany for *Neue Rheinische Zeitung*:

> The French bourgeoisie of 1789 did not leave its allies the peasants in the lurch for one moment. It knew that the basis of its rule was the destruction of feudalism on the land and the establishment of a class of free peasant landowners.

> The German bourgeoisie of 1848 does not hesitate to betray the peasants who are its *natural allies*, its own flesh and blood, and without the peasants this bourgeoisie is powerless against the nobility.

The Prussian bourgeoisie, including the Junkers (the landed aristocracy), used the working people to establish their gains — as in France — but were unwilling to build a new society, fighting to build a revolution that 'leaves the pillars of the old house standing', as Marx wrote in 1844 in *Deutsch-Französische Jahrbücher*.

In both Engels and Marx, we get a sense of the drama of the class struggle, no permanent defeats, but setbacks, no counter-revolutions without new revolutions.

AIJAZ AHMAD: From the point of view of the workers' movement, the proletarian uprising of 1848 was the moment. The February Revolution was actually anti-monarchical, which brought the bourgeois republic into being, or restored the republic. It is the June uprising of the proletariat that united, in a certain sense, all the reactionary classes against that proletarian uprising, while these counter-revolutionary classes and their political organisations were greatly fragmented by their competing interests. There is a long-term counter-revolutionary process after June 1848, which works itself out ultimately in a manner in which the proletariat is defeated anyway, but then each of these various critical forces of the counter-revolution cancel themselves out, and out of which emerges the resolution that comes in the form of the Counter-Revolution. That is where the text ends, where there are these brilliant two or three paragraphs on the evolution of the modern state form of the absolutist monarchy up to the 1850s. That insight gained through the analysis of what went on during the two or three years preceding the coup. These sentences are sweeping and yet, precise:

The executive power with its enormous bureaucratic and military organisation, with its wide-ranging and ingenious state machinery, with a host of officials numbering half a million, besides an army of another half million — this terrifying parasitic body which enmeshes the body of French society and chokes all its pores sprang up in the time of the absolute monarchy, with the decay of the feudal system which it had helped to hasten. The seignorial privileges of the landowners and towns became transformed into so many attributes of the state power, the feudal dignitaries into paid officials, and the motley patterns of conflicting medieval plenary powers into the regulated plan of a state authority whose work is divided and centralized as in a factory.

The *first* French Revolution, with its task of breaking all separate local, territorial, urban, and provincial powers in order to create the civil unity of the nation, was bound to develop what the monarchy had begun, centralization, but at the same time the limits, the attributes, and the agents of the governmental power. Napoleon completed this state machinery. The Legitimate Monarchy and the July Monarchy added nothing to it but a greater division of labour, increasing at the same rate as the division of labour inside the bourgeois society created new groups of interests, and therefore new material for the state administration. Every common interest was immediately severed from the society, countered by a higher, general interest, snatched from the activities of society's members themselves and made an object of government activity — from a bridge, a schoolhouse, and the communal property of a village community, to the railroads, the national wealth, and the national University of France. Finally the parliamentary republic, in its struggle against the revolution, found itself compelled to strengthen the means and the centralization of governmental power with repressive measures. *All revolutions perfected this machine instead of breaking it.* The parties, which alternately contended for domination, regarded the possession of this huge state structure as the chief spoils of the victor.

But under the absolute monarchy, during the first Revolution, and under Napoleon the bureaucracy was only the means of preparing the class rule of the bourgeoisie. Under the Restoration, under Louis Philippe, under the parliamentary republic, it was the instrument of the ruling class, however much it strove for power of its own.

Only under the second Bonaparte does the state

seem to have made itself completely independent. The state machinery has so strengthened itself vis-à-vis civil society that the Chief of the Society of December 10 suffices for its head — an adventurer dropped in from abroad, raised on the shoulders of a drunken soldiery which he bought with whisky and sausages and to which he has to keep throwing more sausages. Hence the low-spirited despair, the feeling of monstrous humiliation and degradation that oppresses the breast of France and makes her gasp. She feels dishonoured.

So there are theoretical formulations prior to this undertaking of writing this text, but learning something from this process. Such as, in the sections above, the way in which classes operate within and through the modern state.

There was not only a Bonapartist counter-revolution. It was not only to create an imperial system, although he became the emperor, and restored the imperial institution; half of France believed that this was the proper role of the state. Louis Bonaparte creates the conditions for the French bourgeoisie to grow not only within the national space, but to move into the colonies. He sets up the situation, in other words, for colonial conquest. Algeria was already conquered brutally in 1830, and France already had many colonial territories in the Americas, in Africa, and in Asia. However, Louis Bonaparte tripled the colonial territories of France, forming a Ministry of the Colonies and the Navy, which meant that the naval fleet was modernised to assist in the colonial conquests in today's Vietnam and Cambodia, as well as in Senegal and other parts of western Africa. Napoleon's great achievement was to take the French Revolution out into much of the rest of Europe and create the environment — as Marx puts it — for which the French bourgeoisie could establish its own stability and its own state, and as a result come to dominate French society. And, as Marx says, once Napoleon achieved this, he was set aside by the Vienna Congress (1814–1815). The nephew — Louis Bonaparte — also saw the solution in expansion, but for him expansion meant to go into the colonies. The French colonial state arose out of that contradiction.

Marx did not know that when he was writing, but there are traces of this insight in *18th Brumaire*. The army, Marx writes, is 'itself no longer the flower of the peasant youth; it is the swamp flower of the peasant lumpen proletariat', and then Marx notes that this army does 'gendarme duty' — but he does not mention that this army does that duty not just inside France or inside Europe, but out in the colonies. This process of colonial expansion is how sections of the peasantry get incorporated in the imperial institution and into the bourgeois interest by expansion of the army into which the Society of December — namely the lumpen-proletariat and the lumpen-peasantry — gets incorporated and then goes into the empire, into the colonies. Many of the problems of class conflict in France are resolved in favour of the bourgeoisie through those processes.

VIJAY PRASHAD: It was not until Marx moved to London in August 1849 that he began to explore the centrality of colonialism to the modern world. He befriends George Julian Harney, in whose paper — *The Red Republican* — the *Communist Manifesto* is reprinted in English. Through Harney, Marx meets Ernest Jones, the leader of the Charist uprising of 1838 to 1857. Jones, who was also German, held firm anti-colonial views, having gone to prison in 1848 for them, views which he published regularly in the *People's Paper*, first published in 1852. When Marx wrote about the Chartists in the *New York Daily Tribune* in August 1852, he used a long quote from Jones about the 'colonial abuses' in Ceylon (Sri Lanka) and Ionia (Turkey). In 1853, Jones wrote of British colonialism in India, calling India the 'Ireland of the East', an expression that tied together the long history of British imperialism. Four years later, when the Indian Revolt broke out in 1857, both Jones and Marx wrote evocatively about both the 'colonial abuses' of Britain and of the possibilities of the Indian revolution ('India is now our best ally', Marx wrote to Engels in January 1858). Marx did not write with similar feeling about French colonialism, although Engels did in his 1857 essay on Algeria for the *New American Cyclopedia* (an assessment markedly at odds with Engels' essay in *Northern Star* in January 1848 that said it was a good thing that Abd el-Kader had been captured and that Algeria had been subdued, since 'the conquest of Algeria is an important and fortunate fact for the progress of civilisation'). In 1857, Engels wrote of Algeria as 'the unhappy country' that had been the 'arena of unceasing bloodshed, rapine, and violence':

Each town, large and small, has been conquered in detail at an immense sacrifice of life. The Arab and Kabyle tribes, to whom independence is precious, and hatred of foreign domination a principle dearer than life itself, have been crushed and broken by the terrible razzias in which dwellings and property are burnt and destroyed, standing crops cut down, and the miserable wretches who remain massacred, or subjected to all the horrors of lust and brutality.

So much for French colonialism and for the progress of civilisation — the *mission civilisatrice* — and for French power. 'French supremacy is perfectly illusionary', Engels wrote in 1857, 'except on the coast and near the towns.

The tribes still assert their independence and detestation of the French regime'. Algeria was the only country outside Europe where Marx visited in 1882, the year before his death. In a letter to his daughter, Laura Lafargue, Marx wrote that the Muslims he encountered believed in 'absolute equality in their social intercourse', but that this social basis of equality in a capitalist world order would 'go to rack and ruin without a revolutionary movement'. I wonder if Marx would have incorporated these insights back into a new edition of *18th Brumaire*!

We have spent a lot of time on these political texts assessing how Marx was a great stylist. Readers often say that *Capital* is difficult to read. I am confounded by this judgment, since I think it is brilliantly written, and that the footnotes are by themselves a treat to read. If a reader is feeling intimidated, I tell them to go to the chapters on the working day and on the machine, both fabulous social histories of British industry. The negative reputation of *Capital* is largely based on the fourth section of the opening chapter, where Marx is exploring the idea of the 'fetishism of commodities'.

AIJAZ AHMAD: *Capital* is a beautifully composed book. When I used to teach *Capital*, I used to start with Chapter 4, on the general formula of capital, which opens Part II of the book and then work my way back to Part I on commodities. If you throw Part I at a person who knows nothing about Marx's political economy, even if that person has done a masters in bourgeois economics, the neoclassical type, that person has no means really coming into that text.

VIJAY PRASHAD: Because that chapter is not really about economics. That opening part is about logic, and logic is an alienating form of thought if you are not comfortable with it. It is about how an elementary contradiction — how two incommensurable things can be possibly exchanged — that he builds the inner kernel of the many contradictions within capitalism, the fiction of money to solve that problem being one of many fictions that hold it together. *Capital* is a fundamental text, but it too suffers from being a source book for random quotations, just as *18th Brumaire* has become a text to extract aphorisms or to use sentences to attack Marx and Marxism. One example, which I already quoted earlier, is the long section on the peasantry, where Marx uses the expression 'sack of potatoes'. Marx is not saying that the peasants are potatoes, but the social fragmentation of the peasantry makes it difficult to produce an authentic political voice for their class. This commentary on the peasantry mirrors Marx's use of the phrase 'idiocy of rural life' in the *Manifesto*. Again, that phrase is wrenched out of context. The exact sentences are useful to re-read:

> The bourgeoisie has subjected the country to the rule of the towns. It has created enormous cities, has greatly increased the urban population as compared with the rural, and has thus rescued a considerable part of the population from the idiocy of rural life.

Marx is not saying that people who live in rural areas are idiots. He refers here to the fact of social fragmentation in rural areas — which he repeats in *18th Brumaire* — and notes that as urban life become more and more complicated and as proletarian consciousness will develop in these congested urban spaces (the factory and the slum), rural peasants will not experience the same kind of rapid transformations. The objective social conditions in rural areas of Europe meant that the peasants would not have the opportunity of trade unions — the school of the working-class — and nor would they have the opportunity of self-conscious participation in the class struggle — the university of the working-class.

AIJAZ AHMAD: The problem of taking random extracts from Marx is even greater about what Marx says about the state at the end of *18th Brumaire*. You abstract that, you just take it out as Marx's theoretical wisdom, without the analysis in which it is grounded. This is a very great problem with reading Marx. Marx is so good at condensation that you can just take that as if the wisdom is contained here. No, that wisdom has been acquired through very hard work of analysis and a fundamental lesson of Marx is that theory per se cannot be applied. You need a very different kind of dialectical operation in order to read the word theoretically.

Even as you get to that phrase — 'sack of potatoes' — Marx has talked about the nature of the French peasantry in the middle of the nineteenth century, when they have all become owners of petty property, too small. He describes it at great length, about how they live; he calls the homes caves, some with one window, others with two windows; he talks about their isolation from one another; he talks about how those holdings are so small that they can only employ family labour and they can't even employ hired labour. This is a sentence about the French peasantry in 1849 and 1850. It is not about peasantry as a whole transhistorically. That is what the problem is here — that it is a very vivid metaphoric statement, a very vivid metaphor. It arises out of some seven or eight pages of describing the peculiar situation of *this* peasantry, not the peasantry in general. And that is what happens when you pick out a sentence from the entire analysis and give it the status of theological truth. You turn Marxism into some kind of theology.

VIJAY PRASHAD: Marx was not, of course, attempting to be

a prophet, but he was analysing society in order to grasp the motion of history and then find a way to intervene on the side of working people for the values of emancipation. 'Philosophy always comes too late', Hegel wrote at the end of *Philosophy of Right* (1820), which finds its echo in Engels' 1895 formulation that it is hard to be accurate in the moment for lack of facts. Indeed, as you say, wisdom is acquired through very hard work of analysis, and you can see that hard work in Marx's letters, his notebooks, his articles for the press, and then in a book like *18th Brumaire*, which brings together that immense labour and condenses it into a lyrical text of great analysis and emotion.

Under the Flag of the Universal Republic

Karl Marx, *The Civil War in France*, 1871

VIJAY PRASHAD: For seventy-two days in 1871 (from 18 March to 28 May), the people of Paris opened the door to utopia. Faced with a ruling class that had led France into a catastrophic war and into subservience to Prussia, the workers of Paris decided to barricade themselves, establish their own government with their own democratic principles, and try to solve the problems that the ruling class had created. 'What elasticity, what historical initiative, what a capacity for self-sacrifice in these Parisians', Karl Marx wrote in a letter to his friend Kugelmann on 12 April 1871.

After six months of hunger and ruin, caused rather by internal treachery than by the external enemy, they rise, beneath Prussian bayonets, as if there had never been a war between France and Germany and the enemy were not at the gates of Paris. History has no like example of such greatness.

These Parisian workers walked on their streets as heirs of the French Revolution of 1789 and of the uprising of 1848. In each of these moments, the workers reached toward the heavens, hoping to create a world designed by and governed by the working people of the world. But, each time, their uprising was taken from them, either by deceit as a small but powerful class — the bourgeoisie — used the mass uprising for their own ends, or by the armed violence of the state mobilised by the government of their class enemies (the bourgeoisie among them). Napoleon I and Napoleon III would become the instruments of the powerful against the aspirations of the many. Defeats in 1789 and 1848 did not stop the workers, who knew that the fight in 1871 would be difficult. It would end with their defeat, with more than 100,000 men and women killed by a ruthless French bourgeoisie.

This seventy-two-day experiment was known as the Paris Commune. It was called a 'commune' because in 1792 the revolutionaries had organised their cities into territorial enclaves that developed principles of local self-government. It was in this tradition of popular government that the uprising in Paris took that name.

Karl Marx watched carefully what was happening in Paris from the Franco-Prussian war of 1870 to the Commune. He delivered three addresses to the General Council of the International Working Men's Association (later known as the First International), first about the war itself (23 July 1870), the second on the events around the defeat of Louis Bonaparte's army at the hands of the Prussians (9 September 1870), and the third — delivered on 30 May 1871, two days after the Commune was destroyed — on the Commune itself. Only the third address was published at that time as a pamphlet. In 1891, for the twentieth anniversary of the Commune, Engels put together the three addresses and published them with an introduction under the title of *The Civil War in France*. This text is the culmination of Marx's cycle of texts on the class struggle in France after the Revolution of 1789–1794 and on how to write about class struggle itself. That's part of the context, but it will need more, Aijaz.

AIJAZ AHMAD: This text — *The Civil War in France* — was, as you say, comprised of three addresses by Marx to the First International, the first two on the Franco-Prussian war and the defeat of the French army, and the third on the Paris Commune itself. The events that led up to the Paris Commune are already in the first two texts, so the third text is much more condensed and a much more theoretical reflection on the Commune rather than a narrative. Engels publishing all three lectures under that title was a good thing to do, then you get all three together.

The first thing to do is to reflect on the relationship of this text with *18th Brumaire*. I actually think that there is a very interesting sequential relation between the *Manifesto*, *18th Brumaire*, and *Civil War in France*. The *Manifesto* is written in expectation of the Revolution of 1848, which breaks out just as it is published. Then Marx writes a number of addresses and essays on the Revolution and its aftermath, which Engels also put together as a collection (*Class Struggles in France*). And then *18th Brumaire*, which is written immediately after the counter-revolution is completed with the coup d'état of Louis Bonaparte. There is an expectation of revolution (*Manifesto*), and there is a defeat of revolution (*18th Brumaire*), and now you have a revolution of a very different order, the Paris Commune which lasts for seventy-two days, in which the proletariat makes a revolution entirely of its own. Unlike the Revolution of 1848, this one is made by the proletariat very self-consciously as a proletarian revolution. They were as much against the so-called Republic led by Adolphe Thiers as a defence of Paris against the foreign power and its troops. And this is a Revolution that actually lasts for seventy-two days.

After the Bolshevik Revolution of 1917 had lasted for seventy-three days, Lenin was found dancing outside the Winter Palace because the Revolution had lasted a day beyond the Paris Commune. In some ways, Lenin thought of the Bolshevik Revolution as the completion or redemption of the Revolution of 1871. So now, because it is a revolution of the proletariat with a certain kind of vision, Marx is now much more interested in what was accomplished during those days. In Section three of the text, as Marx turns to the actual beginning of the Commune, there's just one sentence, saying that Paris woke up to the crises of the commune:

> On the dawn of the 18th of March, Paris arose to the thunder-burst of 'Vive la Commune!' What is the Commune, that sphinx so tantalising to the bourgeois mind?

Then he writes a whole long passage, which is simply lifted from the last section, section seven, of *18th Brumaire*, making it a revised version of the earlier text, the section about the 'ready-made State machinery'. There is an absolute connection in his own mind, and rightly so. The gist of this particular text is Marx's reflections on the fact that the withering of the state is identical to the dictatorship of the proletariat. It's one and the same thing. And how does this state wither away in a movement which is the creation of the dictatorship of the proletariat? How does the proletariat destroy the state, because Marx says that the proletariat cannot merely take hold of it and shape it? He had already made this point at the end of *18th Brumaire*. In the Paris Commune, Marx sees the materialisation of that, and that — I think — is the crux of it for him.

The very phrase, the 'withering away of the state', is something that Marx shared with classical anarchism. And what you saw during the Commune — which Engels was to say much later in the 1880s — is that the followers of Blanqui, the anarchists, were actually numerically the largest in the Commune. The presence of the International in the Commune was not minor. Estimates range from between 50,000 and 200,000 members of the International, although the International was not a disciplined cadre party. You just had to fill up a form and you could become a member of the International. There was no incentive in doing that unless you actually believed in the Programme of the International. So, what you are talking about is a great movement, which had its own organisational structure. Followers of Marx are actually very active in the Commune. For Marx, he was interested in what the Commune actually did in terms of, for example, the restructuring of what in the state of the bourgeoise would be the civil servants, the bureaucracy, and so on and so forth, in which they instituted equality of wages across all jobs. All posts become revocable; everything was by election; the judiciary, which under the bourgeoisie talks of its independence, became an electable office that was open to recall. The creation of a Commune that was the opposite of the state, and this Commune was — in fact — destroying the Republic, the legacy of the various versions of the Republic that had been in France since Napoleon Bonaparte. The whole state structure, the Republican revolution against the monarchy, the most centralised state in Europe after Napolean. To give a notion of an alternative to this centralised state was the task of the Paris Commune.

We call it the Paris Commune, but these developments were not just taking place in Paris. The Flag of the Universal Republic was marched across parts of France. All of France, they felt, would become a network of communes. They were thinking of a certain universality of form of this dictatorship of the proletariat. Their thinking was far beyond what they were able to do over those seventy-two days. Marx does not actually go into the details of what they did, since it was one address. But at the centre of it is that, namely what a socialist non-state would look like.

VIJAY PRASHAD: Not only was it a revolution of the proletariat, but the proletarian character of the Commune must be admitted. The decrees of the Paris Commune clearly show the working class character of its administration: deserted factories were to be occupied and run by the workers, fines levied on the workers were abolished, night work was banned in the bakeries, and church property was taken over for social use. Pawnshops, which had functioned as a kind of security for the working class, were transformed. 'It is well understood that the suppression of the pawnshops is to be succeeded by a social organisation giving serious guarantees of support to the working men thrown out of employment. The establishment of the Commune necessitates institutions protecting the workmen from the exploitation of capital', wrote the Communards.

The attitude of the Commune was that every member of the working classes, including the poor peasants, had to be incorporated into the new society — even those who had fought against the Commune. The chief of the Bureau of Public Safety announced that 'The Commune has sent bread to ninety-two wives of those who are killing us. The widows belong to no party. The Republic has bread for every misery and care for all the orphans'. Madame André Léo of the International Workingmen's Association wrote in her manifesto to the peasants in the countryside, 'Brother, you are being deceived. Our interests are the same. What I ask for, you wish it too. The affranchissement [liberation] which I demand is yours. What Paris after all wants is the land to the peasant, the tool to the worker'. Marx said of these developments, 'It was essentially a working-class government, the product of the struggle of the producing against the appropriating class, the political form at last discovered under which to work out the economic emancipation of labour'.

The officials in the various departments found them to have been run inefficiently by the Empire and set about making them productive. Zéphyrin Camélinat, a bronze-mounter, brought order to the Mint, while Albert Theisz, an engraver, settled the chaos in the postal department (Camélinat was to become the presidential candidate of the Communist Party of France in 1924). There are other names who brought their callous hands to bear on the mess left by the bourgeoisie, among them: Camille Treillard to the Department of Public Assistance, Jules Fontaine to the Post Office, Marius Faillet and Amédée Combault to the Department of Taxation, Louis-Guillaume Debock to the National Printing Press. Elie Reclus and Benjamin Gastineau reorganised the National Library to be used by the people, while Gustave Courbet, who oversaw the Federation of Artists, opened the museums up for popular enjoyment. Their work, over only a few months, showed the efficiency of proletarian governance, the ability of people with dirt under their fingernails to run departments in the interest of all of society, not just for the few.

AIJAZ AHMAD: That is quite right. Marx is interested in these developments, the actuality of the Paris Commune. He is in a hurry to get to them in his text, which is why he rushes there.

Marx quite rightly begins with the Franco-Prussian War and then the reconstitution of the 'fake' Republic. The occasion of the Revolution of 1871 was produced by the crisis of war, namely the crisis of the defeat of France. The vacuum which was created by the withdrawal of the government from Paris to Versailles, the collapse of the army, which was replaced by the National Guard; that crisis opened the possibility. But that crisis was actually not the starting point. Marx quite rightly only talks about that crisis and then goes into the activities of the Commune, and only that aspect of the Commune that is related to the abolition of the state and the rise of the dictatorship of the proletariat. I want to emphasise that because that somewhat resembles the conditions of the October Revolution in 1917, and I think on a global scale it resembles the crisis of a long war from 1937 onward, which made possible the Chinese Revolution of 1949. This chain of great revolutions which come out of that kind of crisis of bourgeois rule. If you only read Marx's text without putting the text in context, the Paris Commune can appear to be a great spontaneous uprising, as if suddenly the working-class rose. What made the organisation of that spontaneity possible is another question that is related to this text.

VIJAY PRASHAD: At several points, you have talked about the abolishment of the state or the withering away of the state and the dictatorship of the proletariat. These are key concepts in *The Civil War in France*, and they become important concepts — through Lenin's *State and Revolution* — in the Marxist tradition. There is a lot of misunderstanding about the term 'dictatorship of the proletariat', but the way you have talked about it is to relate to a far less controversial notion, namely the withering away of the state. A hasty opinion is that the dictatorship of the proletariat would require the hardening of the state and not its withering away.

AIJAZ AHMAD: *18th Brumaire* and *Civil War in France* as well as Lenin's *State and Revolution* are the central texts of the Marxist theory of the state and of revolution. The title *State and Revolution*, Lenin might have taken it from one of the Communards who wrote a book called *State and Revolution*. Lenin's *State and Revolution* is in very large measure a summary and synthesis of Marx and Engels' writings on the state. Lenin writes that there is no reason why we cannot distribute the functions of the state among two hundred million people. That's the dictatorship of the proletariat. Lenin's writings on the dictatorship of the proletariat are fundamentally connected to the idea of the 'liberal' state, the 'democratic' state, which is actually a dictatorship of the bourgeoisie. That liberal, democratic state is a political form of the dictatorship of the bourgeoisie.

The proletariat cannot take hold of the state, but it must smash the state and it cannot then reconstitute the state in the form of the dictatorship of the bourgeoisie. When the proletariat smashes the state, it establishes the dictatorship of the proletariat, which refers to the shift of class power from the bourgeoisie to the proletariat, which is to say, from a minority to a great majority; when the great majority takes hold of the state, it distributes the functions of the state amongst the class as a whole. It is not a state of the minority, and it erects no separate bureaucracy, since it cannot create a state other than itself. The class itself becomes the executive, the legislature, and the judiciary as a whole. The question is what kind of forms you will have. After all, when the Soviets were formed in the early years of the Revolution in the former Tsarist Empire, the 'soviet' is the Russian word for commune. That hope was that this form would be the political expression of the Revolution. Why did it not take that form finally is a different question. At the heart of Marxism is the distribution of the concentration of power that takes place under the dictatorship of the bourgeoisie, the concentration of power in the repressive apparatuses of the state, namely in the army, the police, and the judiciary, which are completely independent of the population at large, even the parliamentary form. This is what needs to be dispersed amongst the classes, and therefore the building of this new state, which is the state of the dictatorship of the proletariat.

VIJAY PRASHAD: *The Civil War in France* shapes Lenin's writings on these issues. He takes notes on this text when he is coming into the new post-Tsarist territory, when the bourgeois government of Kerensky is in power, and Lenin returns to ensure that the revolution does not retreat but in fact advances from a political to a social revolution. Lenin leaves these notes in Finland, and when he eventually gets his notes back, he drafts *State and Revolution*, while the Soviets are being created. It is an extraordinary text because it is written in the midst of the revolutionary escalation, with Lenin at the centre of it, and with Lenin having to escape across the border from Kerensky's police; and because it is a precis of the important texts on the state by Marx and Engels. At the heart of Lenin's text — and this is drawn from *Civil War in France* — is the belief in the capacity of the proletariat to govern. Just before the October Revolution, Lenin drafted a long article for *Prosveshcheniye*, asking can the Bolsheviks retain state power (the text was published on 9 November as a pamphlet after the Bolsheviks took power on 25 October). 'We are not utopians', Lenin wrote. 'We know that an unskilled labourer or a cook cannot immediately get on with the job of state administration'. The key word here is immediately. But then, Lenin writes,

> Is there any way other than practice by which the people can learn to govern themselves and to avoid mistakes? Is there any way other than by proceeding immediately to genuine self-government by the people? The chief thing now is to abandon the prejudiced bourgeois-intellectualist view that only special officials, who by their very social position are entirely dependent upon capital, can administer the state. The chief thing is to put an end to the state of affairs in which bourgeois officials and 'socialist' ministers are trying to govern in the old way, but are incapable of doing so and, after seven months, are faced with a peasant revolt in a peasant country! The chief thing is to imbue the oppressed and the working people with confidence in their own strength, to prove to them in practice that they can and must themselves ensure the *proper*, most strictly

regulated, and organised distribution of bread, all kinds of food, milk, clothing, housing, etc., *in the interests of the poor*. Unless this is done, Russia *cannot* be saved from collapse and ruin. The conscientious, bold, universal move to hand over administrative work to proletarians and semi-proletarians, will, however, rouse such unprecedented revolutionary enthusiasm among the people, will so multiply the people's forces in combating distress, that much that seemed impossible to our narrow, old, bureaucratic forces will become possible for the millions, who will *begin to work for themselves* and not for the capitalists, the gentry, the bureaucrats, and not out of fear of punishment.

'Our revolution will be invincible', Lenin writes, 'if it is not afraid of itself if it transfers all power to the proletariat, for behind us stand the immeasurably larger, more developed, more organised world forces of the proletariat which are temporarily held down by the war but not destroyed; on the contrary, the war has multiplied them'. This sense of the capacity of the people comes directly from Lenin's reading of the Paris Commune and from his own experiences with building the Russian Social Democratic Labour Party, engaging with his close worker comrades, people like Cecilia Bobrovskaya and Ivan Babushkin.

AIJAZ AHMAD: Your reflections take us into what made the Commune possible. Marx quite rightly begins his text with the beginning of the crisis that produced the Commune, a crisis which was rooted in the Franco-Prussian war. But that is not the starting point in actual historical fact. Sometime in 1868, that is to say three years before the Commune came into being, there arose — despite Louis Bonaparte's censorship laws, very strict — a Reunion, an unauthorised, public meeting that does not announce itself as a political meeting. At this meeting, the survivors of 1848 and young workers of France and a number of emigré workers come together to discuss politics.

What can they discuss? They cannot discuss contemporary politics. They cannot discuss the emperor and his state. There is an immediate objective, which is to raise the wages of women workers in a number of factories. Because they cannot discuss day-to-day politics, they discuss high matters. They take the name Commune, because in France there was a commune in 1789. Marx says that on 18 March, Paris arose to the cries of the Commune. But for more than two years, since 1868, all such meetings as the Reunion were beginning with the cry, Vive la Commune, and ending with Vive la Commune! This conception of what the Commune would look like was developed in those clubs, in those reunion centres, which grew all over Paris. These clubs and reunion centres became networks and there were itinerant members of these clubs who would go from one club to the other to create a unity of discussion. They talked about everything that they finally did. This was a real process of working-class thinking at a very high level, making a political breakthrough of its own.

All the details, everything that was being done, had already been worked out, including the form in which it would appear. The National Guard itself had been organised in these kinds of groupings, which brought the whole of the National Guard together. The women's question was very big. When Elizabeth Dmietrieff, the Russian revolutionary and Marx's emissary, showed up first in Geneva and then in Paris, she organised a women's association that played a major role in the Commune, and it became the largest, single organisation in the Commune. This was all done to prepare the ground well before the Commune came into being. It had been thought about before it was put into action. The ability of the working-class not only to organise itself or to rule, but to produce theory at the highest form.

What I am also saying is that what Marx brings to us is in summation what the working-class had thought on its own. Of course, there had been that kind of thinking going on in France for a very long time, and of course, the members of the International were very active, including in those clubs and the reunion centres; they were extremely active in the women's organisations; they were very active in the artists' organisation, which began with a membership of four thousand (these were not artists of 'high art', but actually working people who worked on the artistic sides of production). When the working class becomes the ruling class, it is not the zero point, the start of the process. There has been a very long history of revolutionary attempts, building revolutionary societies. In this particular case, I would argue that just as the October Revolution was prepared by the Bolshevik Party, led by Lenin and his comrades who had conducted a very high level of theoretical discourse as well as organised the Party which was able to lead the Revolution. Something like that had already happened in the case of the Paris Commune, and it was inspired by Marx, inspired by Blanqui, and inspired by others. But the actual practical details were worked out by the workers over three years of preparation. And then they took to the streets on 18 March and yelled, Vive la Commune!

VIJAY PRASHAD: Just a brief note on the legacy of the Commune. The Commune lasted only two months. Over the bodies of the communards, the bourgeoisie of France built an enormous basilica, the Sacre Coeur ('sacred heart'). It was built, the Catholic Church said, to 'expiate the crimes of the Paris Commune'. Today, there is no mention of the grotesque history that sits beneath this enormous building that looks out upon Paris. The bourgeoisie's view of the Commune treats the uprising as a sin and blames the communards themselves for their own deaths. But the revolt did not kill itself; it was killed by the vengeful bourgeoisie, which sought to wrench this hard-fought sovereignty from the hands of the working class and re-establish its order to benefit itself. The democratic advances of the Paris Commune were set aside, their memory erased beneath the basilica. In his preface to a collection of Marx's letters to Kugelmann, Lenin wrote, 'Marx could appreciate that there were moments in history when a struggle of the masses, even in a hopeless cause, was necessary for the sake of the future education of these masses and their training for the next struggle'. The lesson of the Commune was not merely for the Parisian workers or for France, but it was a lesson for the international working class, for our self-education toward our own struggles to overcome the dilemmas of humanity and advance to socialism. Reflecting on the Paris Commune in 1911, the fortieth anniversary of the uprising, Lenin wrote, 'The cause of the Commune is the cause of the social revolution, the cause of the complete political and economic emancipation of the workers. It is the cause of the proletariat of the whole world. And in this sense, it is immortal'.

Selected Writings of Aijaz Ahmad

BOOKS

2004. *Iraq, Afghanistan and The Imperialism of Our Time*. New Delhi: LeftWord Books.

2004. *Reflections on Our Time: Seven Essays on the 20ᵗʰ Century*. Hyderabad: Prajasakthi Book House.

2002. *On Communalism and Globalization: Offensives of the Far Right*. New Delhi: Three Essays Press; 2ⁿᵈ ed. 2004.

2001. *Marx and Engels on the National and Colonial Questions. Selected Writings*, edited, with an introduction. New Delhi: LeftWord Books.

1996. *Lineages of the Present: Political Essays*. New Delhi: Tulika; *Lineages of the Present: Ideology and Politics in South Asia*, rev. ed. London: Verso, 2000.

1992. *In Theory: Classes, Nations, Literatures*. London: Verso.

1971. *Ghazals of Ghalib*, editor and co-translator. New York: Columbia University Press; repr., New Delhi: Oxford University Press, 1994.

ESSAYS

2017. 'The Fallouts of 1989'. In *Interpreting the World to Change*

It: Essays for Prabhat Patnaik, edited by C.P. Chandrasekhar and Jayati Ghosh. New Delhi: Tulika Books.

2015. 'Thinking the Liberal in Liberal Democracy'. In *Democratic Governance and Politics of the Left in South Asia*, edited by Subhoranjan Dasgupta. New Delhi: Aakar Books.

2015. 'Karl Marx, "Global Theorist": Reflections on Kevin Anderson's Marx at the Margins'. *Dialectical Anthropology*, vol. 39, June.

2015. 'India: Liberal Democracy and the Extreme Right'. *Socialist Register 2016*, vol. 52.

2014. 'Alienation and Freedom: Marx's Ontology of Social Being'. In *Marxism: With and Beyond Marx*, edited by A. Bagchi and A. Chatterjee. New York: Routledge.

2014. 'Twelve Jottings on Liberalization of Democracy'. In *Marx, Gandhi and Modernity*, edited by Akeel Bilgrami. New Delhi: Tulika Books.

2012. 'Three "Returns" to Marx: Derrida, Zizek, Badiou'. *Social Scientist*, vol. 40, nos. 7–8 (July–August), pp. 43–59.

2012. 'Nation, Culture, Language'. *Beyond Borders*, vol. 7, no. 2.

2011. 'The Progressive Movement in Its International Setting'. *Social Scientist*, vol. 39, nos. 11–12 (November–December), pp. 26–32.

2010. 'Globalization and Agriculture: Some Propositions'. In *Punjab Peasantry in Turmoil*, edited by Birinder Pal Singh. New Delhi: Manohar.

2010. '"Show Me the Zulu Proust": Thoughts on World Literature'. *Revista Brasileira de Literatura Comparada*, no. 17, pp. 11–45.

2008. 'The Making of India'. In *India and Indology: Past, Present and Future*, edited by Sukumari Bhattacharji. Calcutta: National Book Agency.

2006. 'Debating the Current Conjuncture'. In *Contested Transformations: Changing Economies and Identities in Contemporary India*, edited by Mary E. John, Praveen Kumar Jha and Surinder S. Jodhka. New Delhi: Tulika.

2005. 'Terror, War, Culture'. *Bol*, no. 1 (Winter).

2005. 'The Making of India'. *Social Scientist*, vol. 33, nos. 11–12 (November–December), pp. 3–13.

2005. 'Frontier Gandhi: Reflections on Muslim Nationalism in India'. *Social Scientist*, vol. 33, nos. 1–2 (January–February), pp. 22–39.

2004. 'Indian Politics at the Crossroads: Towards Elections 2004'. In *Will Secular India Survive?*, edited by Mushirul Hasan. New Delhi: Imprint One.

2000. 'Postmodernism & History'. In *The Making of History: Essays Presented to Irfan Habib*, edited by K.N. Pannikar, Terence Byers and Utsa Patnaik. New Delhi: Tulika.

2000. 'The *Communist Manifesto* and "World Literature"'. *Social Scientist*, vol. 28, nos. 7–8 (July–August), pp. 3–30.

1999. 'Class and Colony in Mindanao'. In *Rebels, Warlords and Ulama: A Reader on Muslim Separatism and the War in Southern Philippines*, edited by Kristina Gaerlan and Mara Stankovitch. Manila: Institute of Popular Democracy/ European Solidarity Centre.

1999. 'The War Against the Muslims'. In *Rebels, Warlords and Ulama: A Reader on Muslim Separatism and the War in Southern Philippines*.

1999. 'The *Communist Manifesto*: In Its Own Time, and in Ours'.

In *A World to Win: Essays on* The Communist Manifesto, edited by Prakash Karat. New Delhi: LeftWord Books.

1999. 'The Politics of Culture'. *Social Scientist*, vol. 27, nos. 9–10 (September–October), pp. 65–69.

1999. 'Out of the Dust of Idols'. In 'A World to Win: Essays in Honour of A. Sivanandan', edited by Colin Prescod and Hazel Waters. Special issue, *Race and Class*, vol. 41, nos. 1–2.

1998. 'Right-Wing Politics, and the Culture of Cruelty'. *Social Scientist*, vol. 26, nos. 9–10 (September–October), pp. 3–25.

1998. 'Religio-Cultural Identities and the Nation-State'. *International Dialogue: A Philosophical Journal*, nos. 9–10, pp. 209–28.

1998. 'The *Communist Manifesto* and the Problem of Universality'. *Monthly Review*, vol. 50, no. 2 (June).

1997. 'Postcolonial Theory and the "Post-" Condition'. *Socialist Register 1997*, vol. 33, pp. 353–81.

1996. 'Issues of Class and Culture: An interview with Aijaz Ahmad'. *Monthly Review*, vol. 48, no. 5 (October).

1996. 'In the Eye of the Storm: The Left Chooses'. *Economic & Political Weekly*, vol. 31, no. 22 (1 June).

1996. 'Globalization and the Nation-State'. *Seminar*, no. 437.

1995. 'Postcolonialism: What's In a Name?'. In *Late Imperial Culture*, edited by Michael Sprinker, Román de la Campa and E. Ann Kaplan. London: Verso.

1995. 'The Politics of Literary Postcoloniality'. *Race and Class*, vol. 36, no. 3, pp. 1–20.

1995. 'Culture, Nationalism, and the Role of Intellectuals: An interview with Aijaz Ahmad'. *Monthly Review*, vol. 47, no. 3 (July–August).

1994. 'Reconciling Derrida: "Spectres of Marx" and Deconstructive Politics'. *New Left Review*, no. 208, pp. 88–106. Reprinted in *Ghostly Demarcations: A Symposium on Jacques Derrida's Specters of Marx*, edited by Michael Sprinker. London: Verso, 1999.

1994. 'Nation, Community, Violence'. *South Asia Bulletin: Comparative Studies of South Asia, Africa, and the Middle East*, vol. 14, no. 1, pp. 24–32.

1993. 'Culture, Community, Nation: On the Ruins of Ayodhya'. *Social Scientist*, vol. 21, nos. 7–8 (July–August), pp. 17–48.

1993. 'Fascism and National Culture: Reading Gramsci in the Days of Hindutva'. *Social Scientist*, vol. 21, nos. 3–4 (March–April), pp. 32–68.

1992. 'Azad's Careers: Roads Taken and Not Taken'. In *Islam and Indian Nationalism: Reflections on Abul Kalam Azad*, edited by Mushirul Hasan. New Delhi: Manohar.

1991. 'Disciplinary English: Third-Worldism and Literary Theory'. In *Rethinking English: Essays in Literature, Language, History*, edited by Svati Joshi. New Delhi: Trianka Publishers.

1991. 'Between Orientalism and Historicism: Anthropological Knowledge of India'. *Studies in History*, vol. 7, no. 1, pp. 135–63.

1989. 'The Counterpoint of Pakistan'. In *India: The Formative Years*, edited by Seema Sharma. Delhi: Vikas Publishing House.

1989. 'Some Reflections on Urdu'. *Seminar*, no. 359.

1989. '"Third World Literature" and the Nationalist Ideology'. *Journal of Arts and Ideas*, nos. 17–18, pp. 117–36.

1987. 'Jameson's Rhetoric of Otherness and the "National Allegory"'. *Social Text*, no. 17 (Autumn), pp. 3–25.

1986. 'After the Return of Benazir'. *Pakistan Progressive*, vol. 8, no. 1, pp. 1–25.

1985. 'Class, Nation, and State: Intermediate Classes in Peripheral Societies'. In *Middle Classes in Dependent Countries*, edited by Dale Johnson. Beverly Hills: Sage Publishers.

1985. 'Political Islam: A Critique (Part III)'. *Pakistan Progressive*, vol. 7, no. 2 (Fall), pp. 19–49.

1985. 'Zia's Second Coup'. *Pakistan Progressive*, vol. 7, no. 1, pp. 1–13.

1984. 'The Rebellion of 1983: A Balance Sheet'. *Pakistan Progressive*, vol. 6, no. 1, pp. 1–30.

1983. 'Imperialism and Progress'. In *Theories of Development: Mode of Production or Dependency?*, edited by Ronald H. Chilcote and Dale L. Johnson. Beverly Hills: Sage Publishers.

1983. 'Democracy and Dictatorship'. In *Pakistan: The Roots of Dictatorship: The Political Economy of a Praetorian State*, edited by Hassan Gardezi and Jamil Rashid. London: Zed Press.

1983. 'Political Islam: A Critique (Part II)'. *Pakistan Progressive*, vol. 5, no. 2 (Summer), pp. 3–33.

1982–83. 'Political Islam: A Critique (Part I)'. *Pakistan Progressive*, vol. 4, no. 4 (Winter), pp. 14–42.

1978. 'Democracy and Dictatorship in Pakistan'. *Journal of Contemporary Asia*, vol. 8, no. 4, pp. 477–512.

1975. 'The National Question in Baluchistan'. In *Focus on Baluchistan and the Pashtun Question*, edited by Feroz

Ahmed. Lahore, Pakistan: People's Publishing House.

1975. 'Baluchistan's Agrarian Question'. In *Focus on Baluchistan and the Pashtun Question*.

1975. 'The Arab Stasis'. *Monthly Review*, vol. 27, no. 1 (May).

1975. 'Bangladesh: The Internationalization of Counter-Revolution; Supplemental Remarks'. *Monthly Review*, vol. 26, no. 8 (January).

1970. 'Erikson's Untruth'. *Human Inquiries: Review of Existential Psychology and Psychiatry*, vol. 10, nos. 1–3, pp. 1–21.

1969. 'Ghazal'. *Quarterly Review of Literature*, vol. 16, no. 1–2.

TRANSLATIONS

1979. Six poems translated with W.S. Merwin, in *Selected Translations: 1968–1978*, W.S. Merwin. New York: Athenaeum.

1972. Eight translations with Adrienne Rich, in *Asia: A Journal Published by the Asia Society*, no. 2, pp. 9–13.

1970. Four translations with Mark Strand, David Ray, William Hunt, and William Stafford, in *The Malahat Review*, no. 14.

1970. Eight translations, in *Poetry*, August–September.

1970. Six translations with Adrienne Rich, W.S. Merwin, William Stafford, and Thomas Fitzsimmons, in *Delos*, no. 5.

1969–70. Translations of twenty Urdu poems, with an Introduction, in *The Hudson Review*, vol. 23, no. 4.

AIJAZ AHMAD (1941–2022)

was one of the world's leading Marxist scholars.
His best-known books include *In Theory: Classes,
Nations, Literatures* (1992), *Lineages of the Present:
Ideological and Political Genealogies of Contemporary
South Asia* (1996), and, from LeftWord Books, *Nothing
Human is Alien to Me: Aijaz Ahmad in conversation with
Vijay Prashad* (2020), and *Iraq, Afghanistan and the
Imperialism of Our Time* (2004).

VIJAY PRASHAD

is an Indian historian and journalist. Prashad is the
author of forty books, including *Washington Bullets,
Red Star Over the Third World, The Darker Nations:
A People's History of the Third World* and *The Poorer
Nations: A Possible History of the Global South.*
He is Executive Director at Tricontinental: Institute for
Social Research, Chief Correspondent for Globetrotter,
and editor at LeftWord Books. He has appeared in
two films – *Shadow World* (2016) and
Two Meetings (2017).

www.ingramcontent.com/pod-product-compliance
Lightning Source LLC
LaVergne TN
LVHW041714190726
843493LV00007B/2079